The Aviation No

# Douglas
# DC-6 and DC-7

Stewart Wilson

**NOTEBOOK PUBLICATIONS**
Australia

A view from inside the cabin of Air Atlantique DC-6A G-APSA over a grey English midlands in early 1997. The Coventry based company continues to operate several DCs in various roles.

# Contents

| | |
|---|---|
| The World's Workhorse | 4 |
| Douglas DC-6 | 16 |
| Colour profiles | 32 |
| Military Sixes | 37 |
| Douglas DC-7 | 46 |
| Appendices | 60 |

Published by Notebook Publications, a division of Wilson Media Pty Ltd (ACN 082 531 066) PO Box 181 Bungendore NSW 2621 Australia; fax +61 2 6238 1626.
**Web:   www.notebookpub.com**

ISBN 1 876722 04 5

Copyright © 2001 Stewart Wilson and Wilson Media Pty Ltd

All rights reserved. No part of this book may be reproduced or transmitted in any form or by any means, electronic or mechanical including photocopying, recording or by any other information storage and retreival system, without permission from the publisher in writing.

We state that we are using trademark names and logos in an editorial context with no intention of infringement of those trademarks. Trademarked names and logos, as always, remain the property of their respective companies.

Printed in Australia by Pirie Printers Pty Ltd, 140 Gladstone St Fyshwick ACT 2609. Distributed in the United Kingdom and Irish Republic by Airlife Publishing Ltd, 101 Longden Rd Shrewsbury, Shropshire SY3 9EB England. Distributed in North America by MBI Publishing, 729 Prospect Ave, Osceola, Wisconsin 54020 USA.

Production and design:  Wendy Wilson
Our thanks to the following for contributing photographs to this publication: Eric Allen,  Australian Aviation magazine, John Brooker, George Canciani, David Knott.
Original colour and line drawings by Juanita Franzi

**Front cover:** Ansett-ANA DC-6B VH-INU Kwinana photographed in 1967 immediately before its service with the Australian airline ended after 12 years. (photo: George Canciani)

# The World's Workhorse

The history of the airliner has witnessed some monumental and absorbing struggles for market supremacy and has usually seen the battle come down to a fight between two major players. At the beginning of the 21st century it is between Boeing and Airbus in several market segments; in the 1960s, '70s and 80s it was mainly between Boeing and McDonnell Douglas with the Airbus star rising rapidly in later years; but in the 1950s - often referred to as the 'golden age' of the piston engined airliner - it was Douglas versus Lockheed when the DC-6 and DC-7 were pitted against the Constellation and Super Constellation families in the medium and long range markets.

Since the 1930s, Douglas had been the dominant force in the airliner market with the DC-2 and epochal DC-3, followed by the four engined DC-4 and its pressurised derivative for the post war era, the DC-6. From that was developed the longer range and higher capacity DC-7. The Douglas family of piston engined airliners was developed as far as the *genre* could go - as was the Constellation - before the jet airliners from Boeing and then Douglas revolutionised commercial air travel at the end of the 1950s.

Total production of the DC-6/DC-7 family reached 1,042 (704 DC-6s and 338 DC-7s) between the first flight of the prototype in February 1946 and the end of the line in late 1958. During that period, 872 new aircraft were delivered from the production line to 52 commercial operators in 27 countries. A further 168 went to the US military plus two DC-6As for the Belgian Air Force.

The largest airline customer for new production DC-6s and DC-7s was United Airlines with a combined total of 156 aircraft followed by American (143), Pan American (83), Eastern (50), SAS (36), KLM (32), Northwest Orient (32), Western (31), Delta (28), Sabena (26), National (21), Alitalia (20), Canadian Pacific (19) and Panagra (16).

This list represents many of the world's major domestic and international airlines during the 1950s, but the customer list for the rival Constellation models was equally impressive and included Air France, Air India, BOAC, Capitol, Eastern, KLM, Lufthansa, Pan American, Qantas, Trans-Canada and TWA.

More than 50 commercial operators in 27 countries ordered DC-6s and DC-7s over the years. One of them was the USA's Northeast Airlines which took delivery of 10 DC-6B 'Sunliners' from 1957. This is N6586C, the 849th DC-6/7 off the line.

Some operated both the Lockheed and Douglas products but most tended to be loyal to one or the other. Loyalty to Lockheed was tested late in the career of its aircraft when the very long range DC-7C was put into service just under a year ahead of the final Constellation development, the directly competitive Starliner. This gap and the range benefits offered by the DC-7C was sufficient for several traditional Lockheed customers to change brands, and only three purchased the Starliner.

By then it was largely irrelevant because while Douglas and Lockheed had been fighting amongst themselves for the piston engined market, Boeing had been getting on with the development of the next generation, the 707 jet. When the 707 entered service with Pan American in October 1958 it was all over for the big pistons. Douglas responded with the DC-8 jet but was playing 'catch up', while Lockheed ignored the jet airliner market and instead went with the medium range turboprop Electra.

### The Douglas Heritage

Donald Wills Douglas was the founder of one of America's great aircraft manufacturers, the Douglas Aircraft Company. The son of a New York bank teller, Douglas as a young boy witnessed Orville Wright's early flights, and like many young people then and now, became smitten with flying machines at an early age. After leaving school, Douglas found employment with the Glenn L Martin company in Cleveland, Ohio, working as a design assistant before establishing his own operation in March 1920 in the sunnier climes of California.

Douglas Aircraft's first product, a one-off, Liberty engined biplane called the Cloudster, took to the air for the first time on 24 February 1921.

Douglas headed a small but very talented design and engineering team which included James H 'Dutch' Kindelberger, the man who would later achieve fame at North American Aviation through his involvement in the design of classics such as the T-6 Harvard/Texan, B-25 Mitchell, P-51 Mustang and F-86 Sabre. Later on, another illustrious name in US aviation - Jack Northrop - would become part of the Douglas team before he established his own company in the late 1930s.

Douglas was a major supplier of military aircraft to US and Allied forces

**The ultimate Douglas piston engined airliner, the DC-7C 'Seven Seas'. The DC-7C was developed at the behest of Pan American and was the first airliner capable of routinely crossing the Atlantic non stop in both directions regardless of wind conditions. Pan Am's N732PA *Clipper Blackhawk* (c/n 44874/661) is illustrated here.**

**The first Douglas Commercial. The sole DC-1 first flew in July 1933 as the ancestor of a long line of 'DCs' stretching over nearly seven decades. From it was developed the successful DC-2.**

during World War II, among them the SBD Dauntless carrier based attack aircraft, the A-20 Havoc/Boston and B-26 Invader attack bombers plus the C-47 and C-54 transports. Douglas' wartime efforts also saw the large scale licence production of the Boeing B-17 Fortress and Consolidated B-24 Liberator bombers.

Douglas had experienced considerable expansion during the war. The original factory site at Clover Field, Santa Monica had been joined by new plants at El Segundo and Long Beach (both of these also in California) plus at Chicago (Illinois) and Oklahoma City (Oklahoma).

By 1946 Douglas was a leader in both the civil and military aviation fields, the company's products from the latter group including a lengthy series of naval combat aircraft: the A-1 Skyraider piston engined attack aircraft, F3D Skyknight jet night fighter, the F4D Skyray delta winged jet fighter, the A3D Skywarrior bomber (and its B-66 USAF derivative) plus the compact, versatile and enormously successful A-4 Skyhawk light bomber.

The company's diversity in the years which followed the war is well illustrated by these aircraft and its commercial transports (DC-6, DC-7, DC-8, DC-9 and DC-10), plus its large strategic military transports (C-74 and C-124 Globemaster, C-133 Cargomaster).

Despite this diversity and sales success, Douglas found itself with a cashflow problem in the mid 1960s and looked for an equity investor. It found this in McDonnell Aircraft, manufacturer of a successful series of fighter-bombers, notably the F-4 Phantom which at the time was in large scale production for both the US Navy and US Air Force. A takeover was completed on 28 April 1967 forming the McDonnell Douglas Corporation but the famous Douglas name disappeared completely on 1 August 1997 when MDC was itself taken over by Boeing.

This event saw most of the remaining former Douglas airliners phased out of production - the MD-11 (a stretched DC-10) and the DC-9 derived MD-80/90. One remained, the MD-95 (another DC-9 derivative), this rebadged as the Boeing 717. By late 2001 its future was also in doubt due to disappointing sales and the massive world airline industry downturn which followed the terrorist attacks on New York and Washington DC on 11 September 2001.

**From the DC-1 came the DC-2, the first of the Douglas Commercials to enter production. First flown in May 1934 it was quickly ordered by almost all of the major US domestic airlines and also found a ready export market. A total of 198 was eventually built up until 1939 including 39 assembled by Fokker in Holland.**

### The Douglas Commercials

By the early 1930s the Douglas Aircraft Company had expanded sufficiently and produced a wide enough variety of types to consider taking on more advanced work. Indeed, it could be said that Douglas needed such work, for although its basically simple designs were being purchased in modest quantities, the company was far from prosperous and a shot in the arm was required, both technically and financially.

The opportunity came in 1932 when Boeing began development of its 10 passenger Model 247 twin engined, all metal, cantilever winged monoplane airliner. Sixty 247s had been ordered by United Airlines, and its advanced design features (including retractable undercarriage) made United's main competitors - Trans Continental & Western (TWA) and American Airways (AA) - realise that this aircraft would quickly render their slower and less comfortable fleets obsolete. At that stage the 247 could accurately be described as being very advanced, especially compared to the Ford and Fokker trimotors which were then carrying the bulk of American airline passengers and freight.

To compound the airlines' problem, United's order for the Boeing 247 would tie up production for some time due to the customer's insistence that no others be made available until its contract had been filled. Unable to get this aircraft into their fleets within an acceptable timescale, TWA and AA were obliged to look elsewhere. This seriously inhibited Boeing's ability to sell the aircraft later on, especially since by then Douglas had produced something even better.

It was TWA's Vice President and Chief of Operations, Jack Frye, who first approached Douglas (and the other manufacturers, except Boeing) about

a new airliner and thus set in motion the process which resulted in Douglas becoming one of the world's major suppliers of commercial aircraft for more than six decades.

On 2 August 1932, Frye went to Douglas with a specification for a three engined airliner which was bigger and better than the 247. Chief designer Kindelberger and his assistant, A E Raymond responded with a *twin* engined transport capable of carrying 12 passengers in a two abreast configuration. The powerplants were to be 710hp R-1820 Wright Cyclone nine cylinder radials and the aircraft was of all metal, low wing configuration with retractable undercarriage and such (then) advanced features as split trailing edge wing flaps. A notable feature was the aircraft's extremely strong multi cellular wing structure designed by Jack Northrop.

Design cruise speed was 190mph (305km/h) - some 30mph (48km/h) faster than the 247 and the 12 passengers could be carried over a range of 1,000 miles (1,609km). Important to the specification was TWA's requirement that the aircraft should be able to take off from any aerodrome used by the airline with full load and with one engine inoperative, thus the original request for three engines. The aircraft's maximum take off weight was 17,500lb (7,938kg).

TWA accepted the Douglas proposal and design work on what would be called the Douglas Commercial No 1 (DC-1) began in September 1932. The first Boeing 247 flew in February 1933 and five months later, on 1 July, the DC-1 took to the air for the first time from Douglas' Clover Field facility.

Only one DC-1 was built, the aircraft being used for test flying during the remainder of 1933, activities including the fitting of 700hp (522kW) Pratt & Whitney R-1690 Hornet engines in November (the Cyclones were reinstalled three months later) and extensive engine out performance testing to satisfy not only the authorities but also the manufacturer, the customer and the pilots. The DC-1 represented a radical departure for 1933 and with a length of 60ft 0in (18.28m) and a wing span of 85ft 0in (25.91m) it was also the largest twin engined aircraft built in the USA to that time.

The DC-1 was used for the testing of equipment then in its infancy including de-icing boots on the wing leading edges and propellers, night flying equipment, new navigational aids and a new Sperry autopilot linked to a radio compass.

**The immortal DC-3, the airliner which revolutionised the industry due to its ability to make money without subsidy. Developed at the behest of American Airlines, it first flew in December 1935 and was an immediate success in commercial service. It then formed the backbone of the Allies' transport fleets during World War II and was largely responsible for the regrowth of commercial aviation after 1945. This is VH-AES *Hawdon*, the first aircraft operated by Trans Australia Airlines and still preserved in airworthy condition.**

The original DC-4 (later DC-4E) was a bold attempt to develop an advanced pressurised airliner for US carriers and was partially financed by several of them. The sole prototype flew in June 1938 but after testing and evaluation it was adjudged too big, too complex and too expensive to operate for the times.

TWA took the DC-1 into its fleet in February 1934 (following the presentation of a $US125,000 cheque to Douglas) and immediately proved its superiority over any other airliner flying in the USA or anywhere else. Within days of entering service the DC-1 set a new US coast to coast commercial record (with two stops) of 13hr 4min and followed that with eight new world records and 11 US records for speed and endurance. The point was rapidly being proven, and although only a single DC-1 was built, its successors were manufactured in rather larger quantities.

**One Into Two**

If the DC-1 can be regarded as a kind of 'technology demonstrator', the DC-2 was the production expression of that technology. Delighted with the performance and passenger comfort offered by the DC-1, TWA in September 1933 ordered 20 examples of an improved model to be designated the DC-2. This aircraft was similar to the original in most areas, major differences including the a 24 inch (61cm) longer fuselage which allowed an increase in passenger accommodation to 14 in seven rows.

Initial powerplant was the 710hp (529kW) R-1820-F3 variant of the Wright Cyclone driving two position propellers. Hamilton Standard fully feathering propellers were fitted to later aircraft. The subsequent fitting of 750hp (559kW) Cyclones with feathering propellers allowed progressive increases in maximum weight to ultimately 19,000lb (8,618kg).

TWA increased its order for the DC-2 by a further 20 aircraft in November 1933, and by the time the aircraft recorded its maiden flight on 11 May 1934, 75 examples were on order. Before 1934 was over, all but one of the major United States domestic airlines - TWA, Eastern, American Airlines (out of the old American Airways), Pan American and General Airlines - all had the DC-2 either in service or on order.

The odd one out was of course United, which was for the moment stuck with its Boeing 247s, all of which were converted to the latest 247D specification with improved engines and interiors when the DC-2 came on the scene. But the 247's intrinsic disadvantages, notably its cabin split by the wing spar, its ability to carry only ten passengers and its relatively high landing speed due to a lack of flaps, continued to work against it.

The result was that Boeing was left with an airliner it couldn't sell (just 75 were built) and United had to struggle on with the uncompetitive 247 until it too succumbed to the Douglas onslaught and ordered DC-3s in 1936.

TWA introduced the DC-2 into service on 1 August 1934 and by the end

of that month had taken delivery of all 20 of its initial order. Needless to say, the airline's Ford Trimotors were immediately put to pasture!

A significant number of the 159 DC-2s ultimately built by Douglas (plus 39 assembled in Holland by Fokker) were sold to export customers, the most important being Holland's KLM. Fokker obtained a licence to manufacture the type but in the event it only assembled aircraft for KLM and other European operators including Swissair. The final DC-2 was delivered to the United States Army Air Corps as a C-39 in September 1939.

KLM's involvement with the DC-2 was well publicised in the 1934 MacRobertson England to Australia Air Race. PH-AJU *Uiver* finished second overall in the race behind the purpose built de Havilland DH.88 Comet racer and first in the transport section ahead - symbolically - of a Boeing 247.

**The Immortal Three**

The chain of events which led to the development of the DC-3 came from two different but connected directions, the first a need to improve some areas of the DC-2's flight characteristics, the second an American Airlines requirement for a new sleeper transport to replace the late 1920s vintage Curtiss Condor biplanes the airline then had in service. The Condor was a roomy aircraft capable of accommodating up to 18 seated or 12 sleeper passengers, and the idea was to combine its space with the DC-2's modern features and performance.

The DC-2 did exhibit some flight characteristics which were less than ideal including a tendency to suffer propeller and fin icing problems. It was directionally unstable with the standard fin and rudder, nose heavy, and regarded as not easy to land despite the wing flaps. In addition, its aileron and rudder controls were very heavy and despite previous demonstrations, single engined performance was marginal. From an airline's point of view, more than 14 seats quickly became desirable as the 1930s progressed, as did the ability to operate from New York to Chicago non stop against the prevailing winds, something the DC-2 could not normally do.

Douglas' El Segundo facility developed the 16-22 seat DC-5 local service airliner for operation out of small airports. It first flew in February 1939 and was probably slightly ahead of its time. Any chance of success was thwarted by the outbreak of World War II and only 12 were built.

In May 1934, American Airlines' new president, C R (Cyrus) Smith, and his engineering vice-president, William Littlewood, sat down and discussed the possibilities of a luxury sleeper transport based on an enlarged version of the DC-2. At this stage Douglas was not involved, but Smith and Littlewood did know that Wright would soon have available a new version of the R-1820 engine (the 'G' series) offering 1,000 horsepower (746kW) for takeoff.

Their requirement was for an aircraft with a cabin wide enough to accommodate berths on each side of the cabin for use on trans-continental sleeper services, increased range and a greater payload than the DC-2. A telephone call from Smith to Donald Douglas outlining his needs and proposals got things going, but at first Douglas was reluctant to interfere with the DC-2, which was selling well. Smith pushed the point, sweetening the proposition with the strong suggestion that the airline might order 20 of the new type, ten in sleeper configuration with 16 berths and the remainder as dayplanes with 21 passenger seats.

On 10 May 1935, Douglas submitted its plans for the 'Douglas Sleeper Transport' (DST) to American Airlines; on 8 July, the airline ordered 10 DSTs at a price of $US79,500 each. Soon afterwards, this was amended to eight DSTs and 12 DC-3s.

The DST and DC-3 were simply variants of the same aircraft, the former designation applying to aircraft equipped with sleeper berths and the latter to dayplanes with normal seating. Although the first seven aircraft were completed as DSTs, few others followed and the overall concept of the sleeper DC-3 was largely abandoned.

The first Douglas DST/DC-3 (X14988) flew for the first time from Clover Field on 17 December 1935 in the hands of Carl Cover. Revealed on that day was an airliner with obvious similarities to its predecessor but numerous differences both major and minor. Commonality with the DC-2 was considerably less than the 85 per cent originally envisaged.

The most obvious change was the larger fuselage with its rounded sides. In the DST this space allowed the fitting of eight sleeper compartments each with two berths and separate dressing rooms for men and women. In

**The definitive DC-4 was the immediate predecessor of the DC-6 and DC-7 series. First flown in February 1942, the project was taken over by the US military and more than 1,100 were produced as C-54 or R5D Skymasters during the war years. Afterwards, about 500 were sold or leased by the US military to commercial operators after being refurbished as DC-4s. TWA's N45346 (the former C-54E 44-9124) was the second DC-4 civil conversion, delivered to the airline in February 1946.**

the day version, the DC-3, standard pre war accommodation was for 21 passengers, three abreast in seven rows at a seat pitch of 38 inches (96.5cm) or 24 passengers in eight rows at 33 inch (83.8cm) pitch. After World War II 28 or 32 seat four abreast arrangements were the usual layout.

Two powerplant options were available: the DC-3A with Pratt & Whitney R-1830 Twin Wasps or the DC-3B with Wright R-1820 Cyclones. Power was between 1,000hp and 1,200hp (746-895kW) depending on the engine and its particular variant. The DC-3 entered service with American Airlines in late June 1936 and the order book rapidly increased both from US operators and for export as airlines discovered that here, for the first time, was airliner which could operate profitability without subsidy. It truly revolutionised the commercial aviation business and established Douglas as the major force in the world airliner business.

By the time of Japan's attack on Pearl Harbour on 7 December 1941, 434 DC-3s had been built of which 289 were in service with US operators. A further 369 were on order. The war's needs resulted in military variants of the DC-3 being built in huge numbers - 4,878 in 1944 alone - bringing overall Douglas production to 10,655 by the time it ended in late 1945. To that should be added 2,500 or so manufactured in the Soviet Union as the Li-2 and 485 in Japan by Nakajima as the L2D.

The major military version was the C-47 Skytrain (Dakota in British and Commonwealth service) which provided most of the Allies' air transport capability on all fronts during the war. Post war, the large numbers of military surplus aircraft which became available formed the backbone of the civil fleet all over the world and continued to do so long after newer types had been developed to replace it.

## Four Engines

In early 1936, before the DC-3 had entered service, Douglas and United Air Lines had begun discussing a four engined airliner with twice the capacity of the twin engined aircraft. Design of the aircraft began in February 1936 and the participation of five major airlines soon followed, United, Trans World, Pan American, Eastern and American each putting up $US100,000 to cover the half the cost of developing the aircraft. Between them they also ordered 40.

The new airliner was dubbed DC-4, the redesignation DC-4E (for 'Experi-

**Douglas produced a small number of genuinely civil DC-4s immediately after World War II. VH-EDA of Qantas was one of them, this aircraft originally delivered to Western Air Lines in March 1946.**

The Douglas Commercial series entered the jet age in May 1958 with the first flight of the DC-8, developed in response to the Boeing 707. The company built 556 between then and 1972 in several major versions. This is Philippine Airlines' DC-8 Srs 53 RP-C801, built in 1961.

mental') being applied later when the programme was abandoned and development of the definitive smaller DC-4 (see below) began.

As originally proposed, the DC-4E was a 42 seater with a maximum takeoff weight of 22,680kg (50,000lb) but by the time it appeared the aircraft had grown to a 52 seater weighing 29,484kg (65,000lb) fully loaded, this figure subsequently also increasing slightly. Four 1,450hp (1,081kW) Pratt & Whitney R-2180 Twin Hornet 14-cylinder radials provided the power.

The DC-4E first flew on 7 June 1938 and for its time was a very large and advanced aircraft of all metal stressed skin construction with tricycle undercarriage, pressurised cabin, triple fins and rudders, powered controls and an auxiliary power unit (APU). The fuselage was divided into several compartments including a main cabin, aft stateroom, separate amenities for men and women, a galley and provision for sleeper berths with small windows for them above the main cabin windows.

The DC-4E was awarded certification in May 1939 and handed over to United Air Lines for a series of demonstration and proving flights. It attracted large crowds wherever it went but it soon become clear the aircraft was not suitable for service at that time. It was considered too big for the market, performance was disappointing, operating economics were poor and it showed signs of being something of a maintenance nightmare.

The sponsoring airlines therefore lost interest in the DC-4E, asking Douglas to develop a smaller, unpressurised and less complex four engined airliner instead. The result was the more familiar DC-4 which first flew in February 1942.

The DC-4E was dismantled in October 1939 and sent to the Mitsui Trading Company in Japan, supposedly for operations with Greater Japan Airlines. It was in fact used for a bit of reverse engineering by the Japanese and formed the basis of the unsuccessful Nakajima G5N Shinzan bomber before crashing into Tokyo Bay in 1940.

### Local Service DC-5

Next in line was the DC-5, designed by a team headed by Ed Heinemann

and built by Douglas' El Segundo facility as a 16-22 passenger local service airliner for operation out of minor airports. Perhaps a few years ahead of its time, the DC-5's career was thwarted by the outbreak of war. Of all metal construction, it was the only Douglas high wing commercial transport design and had advanced features such as retractable tricycle undercarriage. Powered by two 900hp (671kW) Wright R-1820 Cyclone radials, the DC-5 cruised at 175kt (325km/h) and had a maximum range of 1,390nm (2,575km). Work on the DC-5 began in 1938 and the prototype first flew on 20 February 1939.

Early flight testing revealed aerodynamic problems include tail buffeting, these cured by giving the horizontal tail surfaces marked dihedral. Interestingly, the prototype was sold to William Boeing in April 1940 as a 16 seat executive aircraft for his personal use as the Boeing company had no equivalent aircraft in its product range.

Commercially, the DC-5 got off to a promising start with orders from KLM (4), Pennsylvania Central (6), SCADTA Colombia (2) and even Britain's Imperial Airways (9) for use on its planned London-Berlin route in 1939. In the event, all but the KLM order lapsed and only 12 DC-5s were built, the

**The last true Douglas Commercial, development of the DC-10 widebody trijet started before the merger with McDonnell but production was conducted under the McDonnell Douglas banner. The first DC-10 flew in August 1970 and the last of 446 in December 1988.**

Next in line was the DC-9 short-medium haul airliner first flown in February 1965. Subsequently developed through the McDonnell Douglas MD-80/90 and Boeing 717 models, more than 2,300 have been built. This is a TAA DC-9 Srs 31. (opposite)

remaining seven aircraft delivered to the US Navy and Marine Corps as the R3D-1 and R3D-2, respectively, before the programme was cancelled.

All production aircraft were built in 1940, KLM receiving its first aircraft in April. Due to the war in Europe, the four DC-5s were diverted to overseas operations, two to the West Indies linking Curaçao and Surinam and the other pair to the Netherlands East Indies operating from Batavia.

### The Definitive Four

After the rejection of the DC-4E by the airlines, attention instead turned to a completely new, smaller and unpressurised DC-4 capable of carrying 44 passengers over medium-long ranges but at considerably lower acquisition and operating costs. Powered by four 1,450hp (1,081kW) Pratt &Whitney R-2000 Twin Wasp 14-cylinder radials, the prototype first flew on 14 February 1942.

Designated DC-4A by its manufacturer, the new aircraft was much more attractive to the airlines and orders for 61 had been placed before first flight, but the events of 7 December 1941 and Japan's attack on Pearl Harbour meant that these were taken over by the US military. As a result, the DC-4 would see no civil service until 1945 and the great bulk of the 1,244 built was of the C-54 (USAAF) and R5D (US Navy) Skymaster models.

Deliveries began in June 1942, the USAAF putting the C-54 into service on regular routes around the world including across the Atlantic to Britain, the Pacific to Australia, the Indian Ocean between Australia and Ceylon and to Africa, China, India and elsewhere. Both Franklin Roosevelt and Winston Churchill used Skymasters as VIP transports.

Post war, the C-54 enjoyed a long career with military and commercial operators all over the world, the latter largely equipping from the approximately 500 sold or leased by the US military to the civilian market in 1945-46. Douglas marketed new civil DC-4s to the airlines after the war but the availability of relatively cheap former military C-54s inhibited sales.

The company nevertheless built 79 as DC-4-1009s, the first of them delivered to Western Air Lines in January 1946 and the last to South African Airways in August 1947. Other customers included Sabena, KLM, Air France, Australian National, Northwest, National, SAS, Sabena, Iberia, Trans Australia and Swissair.

The DC-4 was manufactured under licence in Canada as the Canadair Four/North Star in 1946-49 (71 built powered by Rolls-Royce Merlins) and also served as the basis for 21 Aviation Traders Carvair car transport/ freighter conversions between 1961 and 1968.

The DC-4 was a significant aircraft in the Douglas Commercial series as it was the first of the company's four engined airliners to achieve production and was also the direct ancestor of the DC-6 and DC-7.

# Douglas DC-6

The rivalry between the Douglas DC-6/7 models and the Lockheed Constellation family mentioned in the opening chapter was very much the driving force behind the continued development of both aircraft in the late 1940s and for most of the 1950s. It was the existence of the fast and pressurised Constellation that drove Douglas to begin work on an advanced version of the DC-4 four engined airliner which was in large scale production as the C-54 Skymaster to meet the US military's wartime needs.

The Constellation had first flown in January 1943 but its commercial career had been put on hold due to the USA's involvement in World War II. Instead, initial production was as the C-69 military transport for the USAAF but several airlines were on the list to take delivery of commercial versions as soon as hostilities ended.

Douglas already had pressurised four engined airliner experience with the one-off, 52 seat DC-4E of 1938. Adjudged too large, expensive and complex for the market at the time, the company instead developed the smaller and unpressurised definitive DC-4 which first flew in February 1942, two months after America entered the war. Production was therefore almost entirely for the US military and like the Constellation, commercial use of the DC-4 and its derivatives would have to wait. A few purely commercial versions were built in 1946-47 as an interim measure, by which time the DC-6 had started to enter service.

Douglas had always intended developing a pressurised version of the DC-4 but its incorporation into the more than 1,100 C-54s built during the war years was not necessary. The company had the technology available and the inclination to do it - it was just a matter of the right timing.

Interestingly, there were some pressurised DC-4s built, not by Douglas but by post war licensee Canadair which built 71 in 1946-49 as the Canadair Four or North Star for both military and civil use. These were powered by Rolls-Royce Merlin vee-12 engines rather than the standard Pratt & Whitney R-2000 radials and those for the civil market featured pressurised cabins using a system similar to that installed on the DC-6.

It was against the background of competition from the Constellation once commercial aviation resumed after the war that a Douglas design team led by Arthur Raymond and Ed Burton began development of an improved version of the DC-4/C-54. The company was able to attract US Government funding for the project to meet a USAAF requirement under the

United Airlines DC-6 N37502 *Mainliner New York* (c/n 42867, line no 3), delivered to the airline in November 1946 as part of the first production batch. United eventually purchased 99 DC-6s of all models.

NX90701 (c/n 42854/1) was the first true DC-6, recording its maiden flight on 29 June 1946. After completing its flight test programme it was delivered to American Airlines as *Flagship New York* in April 1947. (Opposite)

The Douglas XC-112A (45-0873), in effect the prototype for the DC-6. Built under a USAAF contract and first flown on 15 February 1946, it was later converted to civil DC-6 standards and enjoyed a long career in commercial service.

title 'Skymaster Improvement Program' which envisaged several variations on the basic design. The C-112, C-114, C-115 and C-116 variants as proposed differed mainly in their powerplants and these are detailed in the 'Military Sixes' chapter of this book.

The end of World War II and the massive reductions in aircraft procurement which followed meant the requirement for such aircraft disappeared for the moment, leaving Douglas with the opportunity to develop the concept for the post war commercial market as the DC-6.

The original July 1944 proposal for an improved C-54 was designated XC-112, this a simple development of the DC-4 combining its unpressurised fuselage with more powerful 2,100hp (1,566kW) Pratt & Whitney R-2800C Double Wasp 18-cylinder radials in place of the C-54's 1,450hp (1,081kW) R-2000 Twin Wasp 14-cylinder radials. This project was quickly dropped in favour of the stretched and pressurised XC-112A.

### From Concept to Reality

Douglas further refined its concept under the designation XC-112A and it was in this form that what was in effect the prototype for the DC-6 series was flown. The XC-112A differed from the earlier XC-112 design in having a 6ft 9in (2.06m) longer fuselage which increased seating capacity from

44 to 52 passengers four abreast. Other external changes over the DC-4 included the incorporation of rectangular rather than circular cabin windows and a taller fin and rudder.

Powerplants were 2,100hp (1,566kW) R-2800-34s (the military designation), weights were increased, an improved alloy was used in most structural areas and systems were updated. A significant improvement was the incorporation of cabin pressurisation, allowing 'over the weather' flight and operations at altitudes which permitted higher cruising speeds and lower fuel consumption.

Equally significant was the fact that the new design created interest among the airlines which had not or could not order Constellations. The Lockheed airliner's launch customer, TWA (controlled by the difficult and contrary Howard Hughes), insisted that none could be sold to competitors on the US trans-continental routes until its own deliveries had been completed.

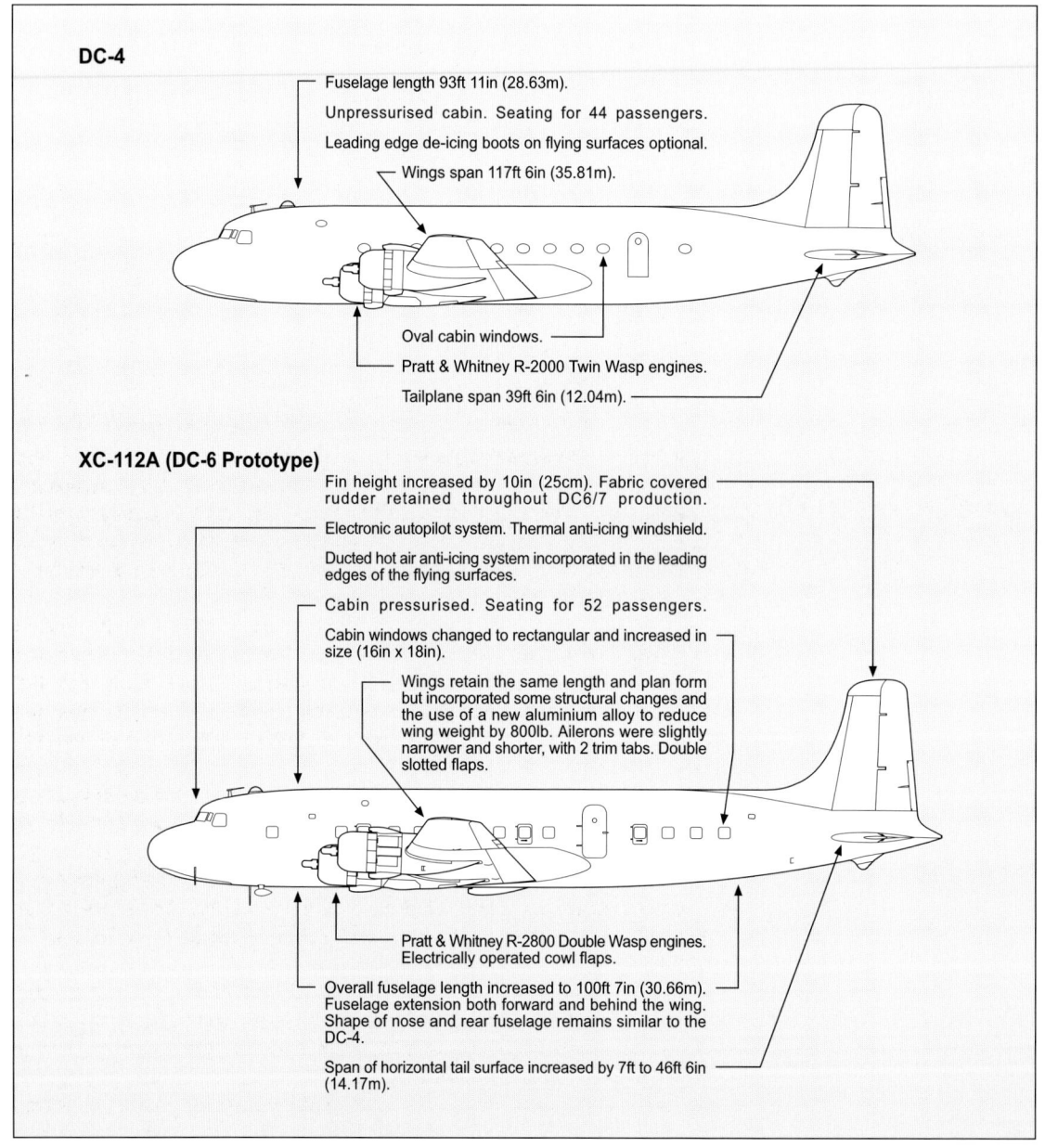

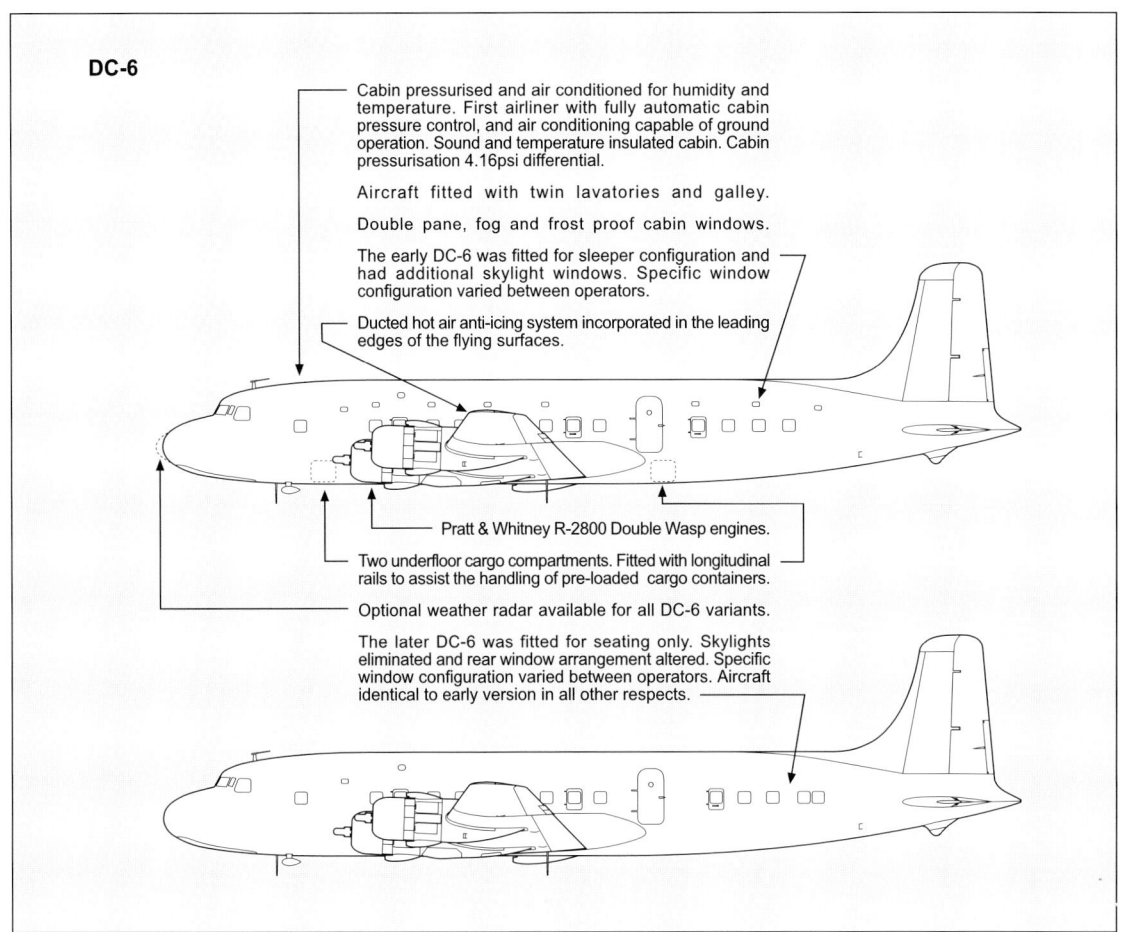

**DC-6**

- Cabin pressurised and air conditioned for humidity and temperature. First airliner with fully automatic cabin pressure control, and air conditioning capable of ground operation. Sound and temperature insulated cabin. Cabin pressurisation 4.16psi differential.
- Aircraft fitted with twin lavatories and galley.
- Double pane, fog and frost proof cabin windows.
- The early DC-6 was fitted for sleeper configuration and had additional skylight windows. Specific window configuration varied between operators.
- Ducted hot air anti-icing system incorporated in the leading edges of the flying surfaces.
- Pratt & Whitney R-2800 Double Wasp engines.
- Two underfloor cargo compartments. Fitted with longitudinal rails to assist the handling of pre-loaded cargo containers.
- Optional weather radar available for all DC-6 variants.
- The later DC-6 was fitted for seating only. Skylights eliminated and rear window arrangement altered. Specific window configuration varied between operators. Aircraft identical to early version in all other respects.

This left the way open for Douglas to sell its new airliner to the others and American Airlines - recognising the need to prepare for post war activities - duly obliged with an order for 50 in November 1944, this quickly followed by a contract for 20 from United. The manufacturer therefore had a sound commercial base on which to develop the DC-6 with 70 orders in the book 15 months before the prototype's first flight.

As TWA's Constellations were ready for service soon after the end of World War II, American and United would be forced to operate slower and unpressurised war surplus DC-4s for a year in competition with the Lockheed airliner while the DC-6 was being readied for service. This was an obvious commercial disadvantage and exactly why TWA had insisted on the exclusivity deal in the first place.

The sole XC-112A (45-0873, c/n 36326) recorded its successful first flight on 15 February 1946 in the hands of Douglas test pilot John Martin and his crew. This was the same month the Constellation entered service on international routes with Pan American and on both international and domestic routes with TWA. Following initial testing the aircraft was delivered to the USAAF on 22 June 1946 and subsequently redesignated YC-112A.

45-0873 was disposed of by the USAF in 1955 and went on to a lengthy career as a commercial transport after conversion to civil DC-6 standards. The first commercial operator was US non scheduled carrier Conner Airlines which flew it as N6166G until May 1961.

Subsequent owners were North Carolina based McDeewill & Street

The cockpit of a DC-6 with the flight engineer's station out of the picture. Note the separate throttle levers for pilot and copilot. Apart from detail changes, the basic layout of the DC-6's 'office' remained constant throughout its production life.

(1961), Spain's TASSA (1963, EC-AUC), M M Landy (1965, N6166G again), Canada's Transair (1965, CF-TAX) and finally Mercer Airlines (1967, N901MA). The prototype's career ended on 8 February 1976 when it crashed onto a golf course shortly after departing Hollywood-Burbank Airport in California following a catastrophic engine failure.

## Technical Aspects

The following is a brief description of the DC-6's main technical characteristics. It applies generally to all models except where specifically noted:

*Wings:* Full cantilever all metal with three spar centre section, the spars permanently attached to the fuselage; outer wings with single main spar; former ribs, spanwise stringers and Alclad skinning. Wing section NACA 23016 at root and NACA 23012 at tip; most of wing structure and skinning of 75ST aluminium; incidence at root 4deg; dihedral 7deg; ailerons and double slotted flaps of metal single spar construction.

*Fuselage:* Conventional all metal circular semi-monocoque (transverse frames and longitudinal stringers) comprising nose/cockpit, cabin and aft sections and covered in Alclad skinning. Cabin windows 18in x 16in (0.46m x 0.41m) hermetically sealed within Plexiglass outer and inner panes; port side main cabin door 72in x 36in (1.82m x 0.91m); flight compartment door on starboard side forward fuselage 50in x 30in (1.27m x 0.76m); two underfloor baggage compartment doors each 37in x 28in (0.94m x 0.71m). DC-6A has two upwards hinging cargo doors on port side of fuselage, forward 67in x 91in (1.70m x 2.31m) and aft 78in x 124in (1.98m x 3.15m).

*Tail Unit:* All metal cantilever with Alclad skinning; tailplane and fin have two spar frames; rudder with single channel spar, ribs and fabric covering; elevators single spar, ribs and fabric covering. Total tailplane/elevator

Mexicana DC-6 XA-MUK (c/n 43121/118) turning around between flights. This aircraft was originally delivered to SAS in May 1948 and Mexicana operated it for ten years from 1964.

area 319.8sq ft (29.70m²); total fin/rudder area 159.9sq ft (14.85m²).

*Undercarriage:* Hydraulically operated retractable tricycle type; main undercarriage units with twin wheels and single shock strut retracting forwards into lower engine nacelle; steerable single nosewheel retracts forward into lower nose; manual emergency lowering system; safety mechanism to prevent undercarriage being retracted with load on wheels; dual hydraulic brake system on each main wheel. Wheel track 24ft 8in (7.52m); wheelbase (DC-6 only) 30ft 8in (9.35m).

*Powerplants:* Four Pratt & Whitney R-2800 Double Wasp geared and supercharged 18-cylinder radial piston engines of between 2,100hp (1,566kW) and 2,500hp (1,864kW) depending on specific variant. Fully feathering and reversing Hamilton Standard or Curtiss Electric three bladed constant-speed propellers of 13ft 1in (3.99m) or 13ft 6in (4.11m) diameter; spinners optional on DC-6A/B. Fuel in eight or ten wing tanks (of which six integral with structure) with total capacity between 3,322 USgal (12,574 l) and 5,512 USgal (20,865 l).

Early production DC-6 (number 13 off the line) OB-R-611 leased by Aerolineas Peruanas and photographed in late 1965. It was originally American Airlines' N90706 *Flagship New Jersey*, delivered in March 1947.

*Accommodation:* Pressurised, heated and air conditioned cockpit and cabin; cabin pressure differential of 4.16psi (DC-6) allows 8,000ft cabin altitude when aircraft flying at 20,000ft, increased differential of 5.46psi on DC-6A/B allows 8,000ft cabin at 25,000ft. Normal flight crew of three on domestic flights (two pilots and flight engineer) or five (two pilots, flight engineer, navigator and radio operator) on overwater operations; passenger

capacity 46-102 depending on model and seating configuration.

Luggage/freight capacities: DC-6 - forward underfloor hold 203cu ft (5.75m$^3$), aft underfloor hold 170cu ft (4.81m$^3$), optional forward cabin compartment 91cu ft (2.58m$^3$), total 464cu ft (13.14m$^3$); DC-6B - forward underfloor hold 267cu ft (7.56m$^3$), aft underfloor hold 242cu ft (6.85m$^3$), total 509cu ft (14.41m$^3$).

*Systems:* 3,000psi hydraulic system for flaps, undercarriage, brakes and windscreen wipers. 28 volt DC electrical system driven by four 300 ampere generators from engines plus two 12 volt batteries in series for auxiliary power; system operated starting, interior lighting and cowl flaps. Hot air anti-icing system on wing and tail surfaces leading edges; electric propeller de-icing.

**Enter The DC-6**

While the XC-112A was undergoing its early flight trials, Douglas was completing construction of the first true DC-6, c/n 42854 line no 1. Initially registered NX90701 (subsequently simply N90701), the first Six recorded its maiden flight on 29 June 1946 and after completing its flight test programme was delivered to American Airlines as *Flagship New York* in April 1947. Its service with American ended in 1961 when it was sold to Aeronaves de Mexico which flew it until 1972. It was then converted to a DC-6F freighter and flown by several smaller operators until withdrawn from use and scrapped in 1980.

Powered by four 2,400hp (1,790kW) with water injection R-2800-CA15 Double Wasp engines, the production DC-6 introduced some airliner design innovations including preloaded cargo containers, an automatic air conditioning system which could also provide temperature and humidity control when the aircraft was on the ground and provision from the start for the fitting of weather radar.

Normal accommodation was for 52 first class passengers four abreast although with the subsequent introduction of 'coach' class seating with reduced pitch this could be increased to around 74 or up to 85 in a high density layout. Douglas offered airlines the option of accommodating between 26 and 39 passengers in 'double decker' sleeping berths early in the DC-6's career (the lower level convertible from and to normal seats) but few operators took it up. The first 100 DC-6s were sold for $US595,000 each, this increasing to $US950,000 for subsequent aircraft.

**Another early DC-6, this time F-OCEC (c/n 42878/19) when operated by Royal Air Cambodge under lease from Air France. This was originally a Panagra aircraft delivered in April 1947 but evidence of another previous owner (Air Liban) can be seen on the lower rear fuselage where the faded registration OD-ACS is just visible.**

The same DC-6A photographed 31 years apart. Late production Liftmaster c/n 45497/995 is seen in Saudi Arabian Airlines colours in July 1966 (with its rear cargo door well displayed) and in February 1997 while in service with most recent operator Air Atlantique as G-APSA. The aircraft was originally delivered to Maritime Central Airways in June 1958, other subsequent owners including British Eagle and Yemen Airways.

Deliveries of the DC-6 to launch customers American and United began simultaneously, the first aircraft for both operators handed over on 24 November 1946. Five months of training and route proving flights followed (while awaiting certification to be awarded), leading to the first commercial services being operated by both airlines on 27 April 1947 by which time they had taken delivery of a combined total of 22 aircraft.

The first American Airlines services were on the New York-Chicago route, the inaugural westbound service conducted by N90701 *Flagship New York* (the original true DC-6) while N90707 *Flagship Illinois* operated the first eastbound service.

Trans-continental New York-San Francisco services were quickly added. Including a single fuel stop, the DC-6 took 10 hours eastbound and 11 hours westbound to complete the journey across the USA, about an hour less than TWA's Constellations and three hours faster than the DC-4. American regularly introduced the DC-6 to new routes as more aircraft became available including New York-Chicago-Los Angeles on 8 June 1947.

United Airlines first used its DC-6s on trans-continental routes but then expanded services to include San Francisco-Honolulu from early May 1947, this the first 'overwater' scheduled service for the new airliner.

Production built up to a healthy rate and by the end of 1947 just under 100 DC-6s had been delivered to the airlines, other operators by then including Pan American Grace (Panagra), Braniff, National and Sabena, the first export customer to receive the aircraft (in July 1947). Panagra

inaugurated DC-6 services on the Miami-Buenos Aires route, Braniff's debuted on the Chicago-Texas route (replacing DC-3s) while National Airlines first flew its DC-6s between New York and Miami in direct competition with Eastern's Constellations. The other major US carrier to receive the DC-6 was Delta, which inaugurated Chicago-Miami services in December 1948.

Many of these US trunk route services were being flown in competition with Constellation operators Eastern and TWA and the rivalry was intense. Although DC-6 operators had not been able to introduce their new aircraft to service for a year or more behind the Constellation. the Lockheed aircraft lost some of its advantage between July and September 1946 when the fleet was grounded after two incidents involving in-flight fires. Just over a year later, the DC-6 would face similar problems.

Overseas, Sabena inaugurated DC-6 services between Brussels and New York in August 1947, while KLM Royal Dutch Airlines - a major Constellation operator - also took delivery of eight DC-6s from August 1948, initially for use on its Amsterdam-Tehran service. Other major international airlines which would receive DC-6s over the next few years included Aerolineas Argentinas, Linee Aeree Italiane (LAI - later merged with Alitalia), Mexicana, Philippine Air Lines and Scandinavian Airlines System (SAS).

By 1950 DC-6 production was down to a relative trickle as most orders had been filled (only three were delivered in 1949 and 17 in 1950) and the improved DC-6B was still more than a year away from entering service. The 174th and last DC-6 (N6889, c/n 43295/205) was delivered to Braniff on 2 November 1951. By then, DC-6B deliveries had been underway for seven months and the stretched Lockheed Super Constellation was only a month away from entering service.

**Problems and Records**

Although the DC-6 went on to have a long, successful and generally safe career, its early service was marred by the grounding of the fleet for over four months while the causes of two incidents were being investigated.

On 24 October 1947 United Airlines DC-6 N37510 *Mainliner Seattle* crashed in flames in the Bryce Canyon National Park, Utah, killing all 52

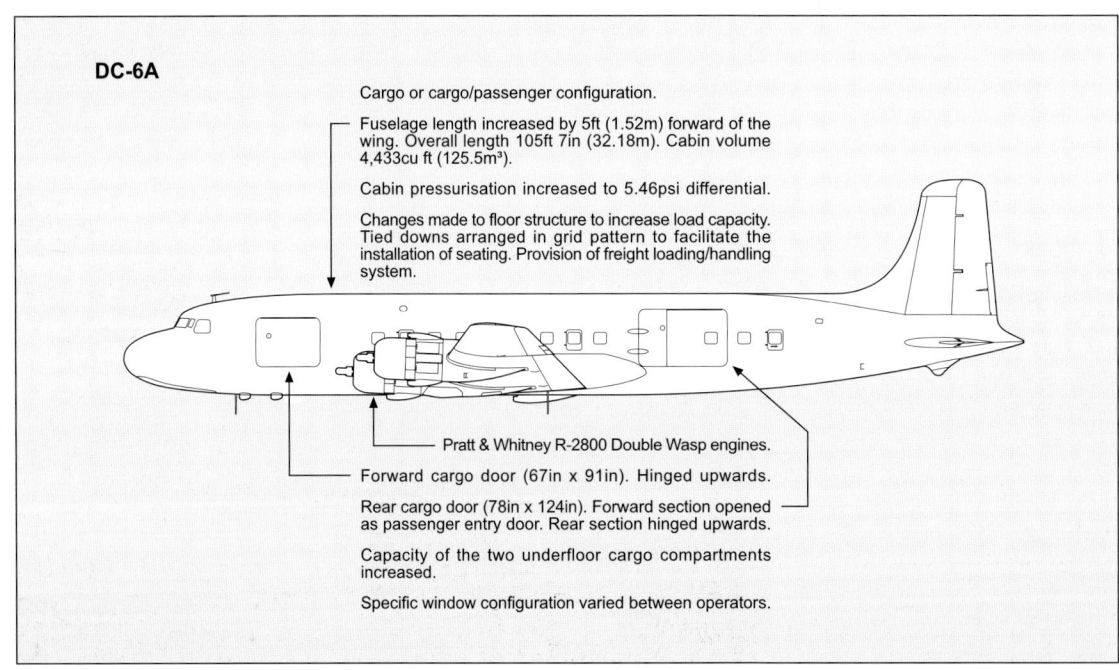

DC-6A

Cargo or cargo/passenger configuration.

Fuselage length increased by 5ft (1.52m) forward of the wing. Overall length 105ft 7in (32.18m). Cabin volume 4,433cu ft (125.5m³).

Cabin pressurisation increased to 5.46psi differential.

Changes made to floor structure to increase load capacity. Tied downs arranged in grid pattern to facilitate the installation of seating. Provision of freight loading/handling system.

Pratt & Whitney R-2800 Double Wasp engines.

Forward cargo door (67in x 91in). Hinged upwards.

Rear cargo door (78in x 124in). Forward section opened as passenger entry door. Rear section hinged upwards.

Capacity of the two underfloor cargo compartments increased.

Specific window configuration varied between operators.

passengers and crew on board. Less than three weeks later, on 11 November, an American Airlines DC-6 also suffered an in-flight fire but this time the crew was able to make a successful emergency landing at Gallup, New Mexico. The DC-6 fleet was grounded the next day.

Investigations eventually revealed that under some circumstances, fuel could overflow from the tank vents straight into the cabin heater intake located in the belly hold, with potentially catastrophic results. Modifications were devised and incorporated but it wasn't until 21 March 1948 that the DC-6 was cleared to fly again. The intervening period was expensive for both the airlines and Douglas, which had to carry the cost of the modifications.

After that, things settled down for the DC-6 which quickly proved itself to be reliable and economical to operate. It was also responsible for the setting of several speed records for its class between city pairs, these summarised below:

| Date | Cities | Airline | Time | Average Speed |
|---|---|---|---|---|
| 4 Oct 1948 | LA-Jacksonville | Delta | 6hr 43min | 320mph (516km/h) |
| 3 June 1947 | Los Angeles-Tampa | National | 6hr 05min | 354mph (570km/h) |
| 3 June 1947 | Tampa-Miami | National | 0hr 39min | 312mph (502km/h) |
| 23 Oct 1948 | Los Angeles-Atlanta | Delta | 6hr 11min | 313mph (504km/h) |
| 6 Nov 1948 | LA-Charleston | Delta | 6hr 24min | 344mph (554km/h) |
| 2 Mar 1950 | Chicago-Miami | Delta | 3hr 08min | 376mph (605km/h) |
| 3 Dec 1950 | LA-Mexico City | Mexicana | 4hr 12min | 370mph (595km/h) |

By 1960 several of the major US airlines had already begun retiring their DC-6s and selling them to other operators, although some kept a number of aircraft until the late 1960s for use on shorter haul routes and fitted with high density seating. Many European airlines began disposing of their DC-6s at around the same time. Some of these used aircraft went to airlines which had purchased new aircraft and wished to top up their fleets but most went to secondary operators all over the world, sometimes starting a chain of sales and resales which saw many DC-6s pass through the hands of numerous owners before being finally retired. Some ended up in military service and others were converted to freighters.

An example of an individual DC-6 with a long history of diverse ownership is Braniff's N90883 (c/n 43107, l/no 93), first delivered in October 1947. It was disposed of in 1966 to La Jolla Associates (which leased it to Mexicana) and subsequent owners and lessees were William J Brennan, Frances U Brennan, the United National Bank, Bellomy-Lawson Aviation

**Bayu Indonesia Air DC-6A PK-BAT (c/n 44420/479) photographed in 1978, this side view well showing the placement of the fore and aft cargo doors. Originally built for Sabena in 1954, this aircraft ended its days by crashing into the sea near Bimini Island in the Bahamas.**

(which had it converted to a DC-6F freighter), Caraibische Lucht Transport, Pan African Airlines, Lloyd Aero Corporation, Carolina Aircraft Corporation and finally Florida Aircraft Leasing in 1982. In the mid 1980s '93' was withdrawn from service and relegated to non flying engine test bed activities.

**DC-6A Liftmaster**

The availability of the 'CB' series of Pratt & Whitney R-2800 Double Wasp engines allowed Douglas to develop stretched and heavier versions of the basic DC-6. A 1.52m (5ft 0in) longer fuselage provided space for an extra two rows of seating in the passenger version (DC-6B) but it was the DC-6A Liftmaster freighter which appeared first as Douglas had an eye on the potentially lucrative military market for this aircraft through US Air Force and Navy orders.

Development of the DC-6A was approved in January 1948 and the first example (N3006, c/n 42901/153) flew on 29 September 1949, 17 months before the DC-6B. Despite this, the first DC-6A was not delivered until April 1951 due to slow sales, a few days after the first DC-6B was handed over. Two more were delivered later in 1951 but regular deliveries didn't start until early 1953 due to a lack of orders, this probably a function of the DC-6A's selling price of $US1.25 million at a time when many operators could find suitable second hand aircraft (notably DC-4s) at a fraction of that cost.

Compared to the original DC-6, the Liftmaster featured 2,400hp (1,790kW) R-2800-CB16 or 2,500hp (1,864kW) CB17 Double Wasp engines driving three bladed propellers of slightly larger diameter. The longer fuselage incorporated structural strengthening to allow a 9,800lb (4,445kg) increase in maximum takeoff weight to 107,000lb (48,535kg), most of which was available for additional useful load. The maximum zero fuel weight (above which all load must be in fuel) was also substantially increased to allow a payload increase of 38 per cent to around 29,500lb (13,380kg), while several optional fuel capacities were offered up to a maximum of 5,512 US gal (20,865 l) or 17 per cent more than the maximum available on the DC-6.

The DC-6A's optimisation for freight operations saw the fitting of numerous specialist features including large upwards opening cargo doors forward and aft of the wing on the port side of the fuselage, the cabin windows were covered with metal plugs, the main cabin floor was strengthened to

**The DC-6B was numerically the most successful of any DC-6/7 variant with 288 built, airlines discovering that on a seat-mile cost basis, it was arguably the most economical piston engined airliner ever built. N8221H (c/n 43738/277) was one of eight DC-6Bs delivered to National Airlines (the 'Airline of the Stars') between October 1952 and January 1953.**

**Western Air Lines was a major DC-6B customer, taking delivery of 31 from November 1952. N93117 (c/n 45060/725) was from a later batch, delivered in October 1956.**

withstand a static load of 200lb/sq ft, floor tie downs were incorporated, there was an optional built in power lift system for the loading and unloading of freight and special racks were available for the bulk shipping of garments. Total cargo volume (including the two underfloor holds) was 5,000 cubic feet (141.6m$^3$).

Some carriers later operated their DC-6As in a 'quick change' configuration in which the passenger windows were restored so the interior could be converted to passenger configuration when traffic conditions required. The DC-6C (see below) was built to this standard from the start, as were the US Military's C-118/R6Ds.

The first Liftmaster was also the first delivered to a customer, Slick Airways on 16 April 1961 with the new registration N90806. Slick received two more later in 1951 and another three in early 1953, this marking the start of more regular DC-6A deliveries, the aircraft built in parallel with the C-118/R6D military versions which had been ordered in substantial quantities.

Subsequent customers included American Airlines (for use on its long haul freight routes), the Belgian Air Force, Canadian Pacific, Flying Tiger Line (almost all of which were immediately leased out to other operators), KLM, Pan Am and United plus several other scheduled and supplemental carriers which purchased the aircraft in ones and twos.

Like the DC-6, the DC-6A also set some records including a couple of city-to-city speed records for commercial freight transports plus a more significant one in May 1951 when a Slick Airways Liftmaster established a new world record for the largest single piece of cargo ever airlifted to that point, a 10,430kg (23,000lb) extrusion press carried from Philadelphia to Los Angeles.

The 67th and last DC-6A (c/n 45369/984) was delivered to Trans Caribbean Airlines as N6541C on 6 October 1958, bringing total production of the Liftmaster series (including 166 military versions and seven DC-6Cs) to 240 aircraft.

Even though demand for new DC-6As had not been overwhelming, once it was out of production second hand examples were eagerly sought by operators who could then afford its lower capital cost and were attracted by its good operating economics. DC-6As changed hands frequently over the years, appearing in the fleets of freight and second tier carriers all over the world. Only two were sold new to a military operator (Belgium) but

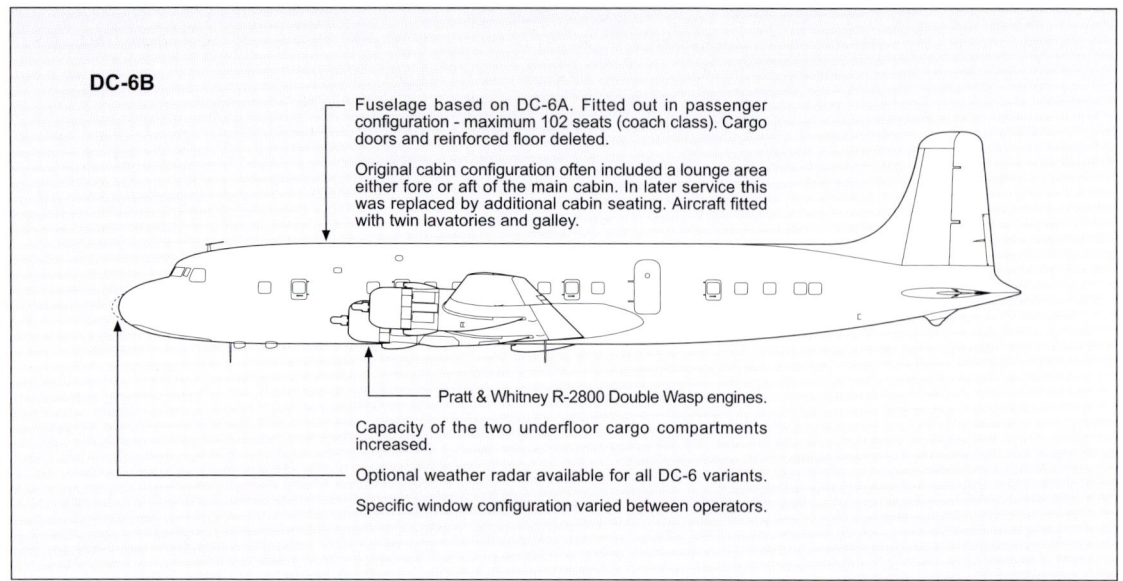

another 11 eventually found their way into military service.

Two interesting second hand acquisitions were the aircraft obtained in 1960 by the US Department of Commerce for operation by the Weather Bureau. Purchased from Trans Caribbean Airways (N6539C c/n 45227/900 and N6540C c/n 45368/932) they were fitted with radar and instrumentation appropriate for their role as part of the Bureau's hurricane research programme.

## DC-6B

The most commercially successful of all the DC-6 variants with 288 built for 32 operators in 20 countries, the DC-6B was a passenger carrying version of the DC-6A Liftmaster freighter. It combined the DC-6A's R-2800-CB16/17 powerplants, increased fuel capacity options, 5ft 0in (1.52m) longer fuselage, higher operating weights and other mechanical features

**Capital Airlines didn't purchase any new DC-6Bs but leased 11 from Pan Am in 1960-61 to cover capacity lost when 15 Vickers Viscounts were repossessed by the manufacturer after the airline ran into financial difficulties. N6523C (c/n 43523/230) was one of them.**

with a passenger interior. The DC-6A's specialist freighter equipment - large cargo doors, reinforced cabin floor etc - was deleted.

The result was what many consider to be the finest piston engined airliner ever built due to its combination of performance, passenger appeal and operating economics which featured seat-mile costs lower than any other airliner with reciprocating engines. The DC-6B was built largely in response to Lockheed's continual upgrading of its Constellation models, simultaneously offering the increased passenger capacity and greater range the airlines were asking for. Its long list of customers included most of those which had operated the original DC-6 plus many new buyers.

Perhaps strangely, the DC-6B was not formally offered to the market until January 1950, two years after the mechanically identical DC-6A was launched. With standard DC-6 production winding down by then, the programme needed a boost and the DC-6B provided that. Major DC-6B customers included Alitalia (10), American Airlines (25), Canadian Pacific (13), Northeast (10), Northwest Orient (12), Pan American (45), SAS (14), United (44) and Western (31).

Several of these were new Douglas customers while Douglas stalwarts who ordered smaller quantities of DC-6Bs to supplement their earlier aircraft included KLM, Mexicana, National, PAL, Sabena and Swissair. Some were especially significant as they had previously been Constellation operators. Pan American, for example replaced its early model L.049 and L.749 Constellations with DC-6Bs for use on the New York-London route instead of opting for the Super Constellation, while the 'B' introduced the DC-6 to the fleets of several US trunk route operators for the first time, among them Continental, Northeast, Northwest Orient and Western. Even Eastern Air Lines - which ordered more than 60 Constellations and Super Constellations over the years - operated seven leased DC-6Bs for a period and also purchased a large fleet of DC-7Bs.

Two DC-6B models were offered to the airlines: Domestic and Overwater.

Cathay Pacific's sole DC-6B, VR-HFK (c/n 45496/992). The aircraft was delivered new to the Hong Kong airline in June 1958, supplementing an ex Pan Am DC-6 it had acquired in 1955.

The Domestic version was intended largely for US trans-continental services and generally utilised a maximum takeoff weight of 100,000lb (45,360kg) along with a fuel capacity which was less than the maximum available. Flight crew was normally three (two pilots and flight engineer) passenger accommodation ranged from typically 60-66 in early first class layouts, increasing to 82 economy class passengers or up to 102 in later high density configurations. List price was $US1.12 million.

The Overwater models took advantage of the maximum available fuel capacity of 5,512 USgal (20,865 l) and an increase in maximum weight to 107,000lb (48,535kg) for long range operations. The flight crew normally increased to five with the addition of a navigator and radio operator, while passenger accommodation was typically around 54-60 in the days when there was only first class seating on international airliners. The DC-6B Overwater initially sold for $US1.47 million.

Despite its extra range, the DC-6B Overwater still couldn't achieve the 'Holy Grail' of routine non stop trans-Atlantic operations in both directions with westbound flights against the prevailing wind normally requiring a fuel stop if the necessary reserves were to be preserved. This capability remained unavailable from any Douglas (and Lockheed) airliner until the 'ultimate pistons' - the DC-7C and Starliner - were developed.

The first DC-6B (N37547, c/n 43257/174) was flown on 2 February 1951 and deliveries to United Airlines began on 11 April when N37549 *Mainliner Detroit* was handed over. Four others (including the first aircraft)

**Former Northwest Orient DC-6B N581 (c/n 45501/953) in the colours of its second owner, Finland's Kar-Air as OH-KDB. Kar-Air purchased the aircraft in February 1965.**

**Egyptian registered DC-6B SU-ANO (c/n 45320/930) of United Arab Airlines, photographed in July 1966, a year after it was purchased from original owner Northwest Orient. It later flew with Sweden's Sterling Airways and the United Nations.**

When Australia's Ansett Airways merged with Australian National Airways to form Ansett-ANA in October 1957 it acquired DC-6B VH-INS (c/n 45076/712) which had been delivered just over a year earlier. It is photographed at Sydney's Mascot Airport in June 1965.

Iceland's Fragtflug purchased this ex Western Air Lines/Japan Air Lines DC-6B (c/n 45060/725) in May 1969 as TF-FRA and leased it to UNICEF for use by the International Red Cross as part of the Biafran relief effort.

were in United's hands by the end of the month. Deliveries to American Airlines also started in April 1951 followed by Swissair in June and Braniff in August. Airlines which added the DC-6B to their fleets in 1952-53 included Canadian Pacific, Continental, KLM, Mexicana, Pan American, Panagra, PAL, Sabena, SAS, TAI and Western.

The DC-6B added to the achievements of its forebears by setting several records including the longest non stop commercial flight at the time, the 4,950nm (9,170km) between Los Angeles and Paris. This was achieved in May 1953 by a Transportes Aeriens Intercontinentaux (TAI) aircraft. An SAS DC-6B (OY-KME c/n 43744/288 *Arild Viking*) completed the first commercial flight over the North Pole from Los Angles to Copenhagen via Greenland on 18 November 1952 during its delivery flight.

The last DC-6B built was YU-AFB (c/n 45564/1040), handed over to Jugoslovenski Aerotransport (JAT) on 17 November 1958, but the final delivery took place on 12 December when SX-DAI *Isle of Kreta* (c/n 45544/1026) was taken into Olympic Airways' fleet.

### DC-6C

The last seven Liftmasters were built to DC-6C standards, this fundamentally a 'quick change' version of the DC-6A in which the aircraft could be quickly converted from a freight carrier to a passenger transport or *vice-versa*. Several DC-6As were converted to DC-6C standards and the C-118s and R6Ds built for the US military had similar capability.

Despite being announced by Douglas in June 1953, it would be another

Copyright© 2001 Juanita Franzi

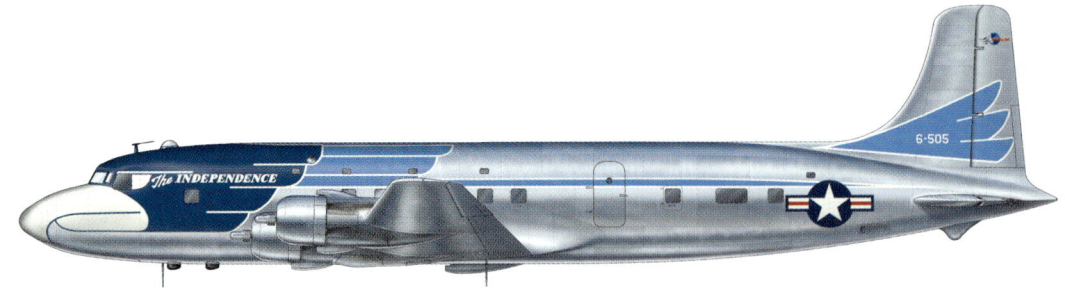

VC-1184 6-0505 *The Independence* (c/n 42881/29) USAF late 1947; presidential transport of Harry S Truman.

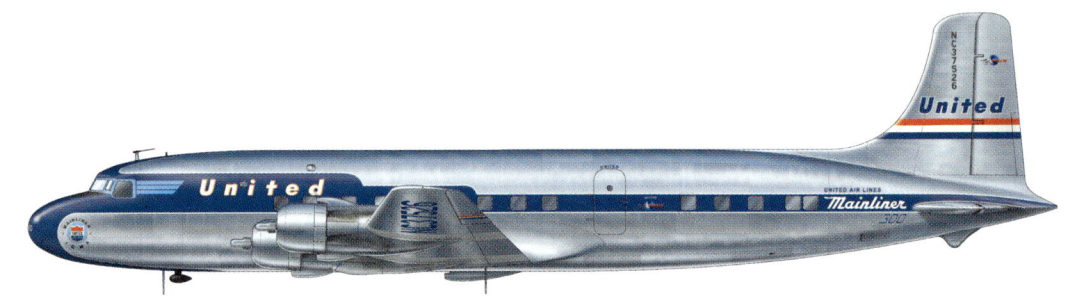

DC-6 NC37526 *Mainliner Iowa* (c/n 43015/65), United Air Lines 1948.

DC-6A N6814C (c/n 45058/662), Slick Airways 1957.

DC-6B VH-INH (c/n 44693/551), Trans Australia Airlines; leased from Ansett-ANA 1960-66.

Copyright© 2001 Juanita Franzi

DC-7 N8206H (c/n 44172/421), National Airlines 1954.

DC-7B N8211H *City of Los Angeles* (c/n 45194/791), Continental Airlines 1958.

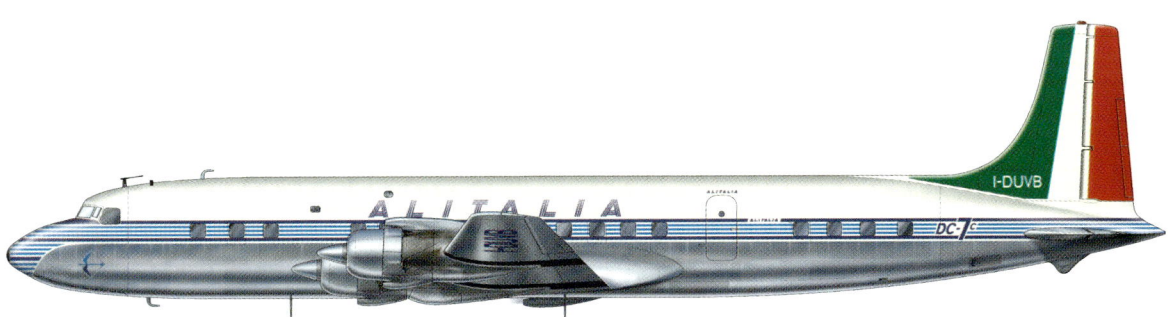

DC-7C I-DUVB (c/n 45542/1009), Alitalia 1958.

DC-7C N731PA *Clipper Bald Eagle* (c/n 44873/656), Pan American World Airways; first in fleet November 1956.

five years before any DC-6Cs were built, the first aircraft (c/n 45481/991) delivered to Lebanon's Air Liban on 5 June 1958. The remaining six were delivered to Britain's Hunting Clan Air Transport (2) and Brazil's Loide Aereo Nacional (4). A Loide aircraft (PP-LFC, c/n 45529/1035) had special significance as it was the final DC-6 of any model to be delivered, on 10 February 1959. All four of Loide's DC-6Cs were leased to Panair do Brasil immediately after delivery.

### DC-6 Conversions

More than 90 DC-6s were converted to freighters or convertible passenger/freight aircraft, Douglas first offering such a programme in 1958 for both DC-6 and DC-7 operators. Many were performed under licence to Douglas by California based Pacific Airmotive Corporation until well into the 1970s,

**Unpainted SE-BDG (c/n 45329/853) of Transair Sweden with radar installation under the forward fuselage. Transair purchased this aircraft from original owner Canadian Pacific in late 1961.**

Trans Australia Airlines DC-6B VH-TAD (c/n 44687/535, opposite) was one of the many Sixes converted to freighters, in this case a DC-6AB convertible passenger/freight version. The outline of the two cargo doors can be made out in this April 1966 shot of the aircraft departing Sydney Airport.

The DC-6 and DC-7 found widespread use as firebombers and insect sprayers in North America and elsewhere, operated by the US Forest Service, Canada's Conair and others. Conair also developed systems for the DCs and other aircraft and performed the conversions. A DC-6B could be fitted with a 3,000 USgal (11,356 l) tank, its 12 microcomputer controlled release doors allowing considerable flexibility when dropping the water/retardant mix.

while several other organisations performed 'unofficial' conversions.

Douglas itself undertook the early conversions, the last of about 70 for 15 airlines (including DC-7s) rolling out of its famous Clover Field, Santa Monica facility in November 1962. These were the final aircraft to emerge from the factory which had been in operation for 40 years. It was subsequently used for building space vehicles and missiles until 1975 when it was closed.

The conversions involved the fitting of large cargo doors and reinforced cabin floors plus the necessary freight handling equipment. Some had their cabin windows blanked out in a similar fashion to the DC-6A Liftmaster but others retained the widows as they were converted to a standard similar to the 'quick change' DC-6C.

A number of the conversions ended up in military service including with the air forces of Argentina, Chile, El Salvador, France, West Germany, Guatemala, Mexico and Portugal (see 'Military Sixes' chapter for details). Most of the approximately 90 DC-6s which were still in service by late 2001 were freighter or quick change models created by conversion.

Various new designations were applied to converted aircraft:

**DC-6F:** 12 DC-6s converted to freighters. One other was redesignated 'DC-6A' after an unofficial conversion but it did not feature the lengthened fuselage, increased weights and more powerful engines of that model.

**DC-6AB:** 39 DC-6Bs converted to a 'quick change' passenger/freight standard similar to the DC-6C.

**DC-6BF:** 40 DC-6Bs converted to pure freighters, similar to the DC-6A.

**DC-6B-ST:** Also known as the DC-6BF Swingtail, two DC-6Bs were modified to 'swingtail', freighters by Sabena's engineering section. These aircraft featured rear fuselages which were hinged so as to swing to one side to facilitate the easy loading of long or bulky objects. The first, EC-BBK (c/n 44434/516) of Spain's Spantax was converted in August 1965; the second conversion was completed in April 1968 for Finland's Kar-Air on OH-KDA (c/n 45202/880).

## DOUGLAS DC-6

**Powerplants:** DC-6 - four 2,100hp (1,566kW) dry/2,400hp (1,790kW) with water injection Pratt & Whitney R-2800-CA15 Double Wasp 18-cylinder radials; Hamilton Standard three bladed propellers of 13ft 1in (3.99m) diameter. Fuel capacity 3,322-4,700 USgal (12,575-17,790 l).

DC-6A/B - four 2,400hp (1,790kW) with water injection Pratt & Whitney R-2800-CB16 or 2,500hp (1,864kW) R-2800-CB17 Double Wasp 18-cylinder radials; Hamilton Standard or Curtiss Electric three bladed propellers of 13ft 6in (4.11m) diameter. Fuel capacity 3,992-5,512 USgal (15,110-20,865 l).

**Dimensions:** DC-6 - wing span 117ft 6in (35.81m); length 100ft 7in (30.66m); height 28ft 8in (8.74m); wing area 1,463sq ft (135.9m$^2$).

DC-6A/B - length 105ft 7in (32.18m).

**Weights:** DC-6 - typical empty 53,623lb (24,323kg); max takeoff 97,200lb (44,090kg); max landing 80,000lb (36,288kg); max payload 21,300lb (9,662kg).

DC-6A - empty 51,300lb (23,270kg); max takeoff 107,000lb (48,535kg); max landing 88,200lb (40,007kg); max payload 29,500lb (13,381kg).

DC-6B (Domestic/Overwater) - typical empty 55,350lb (25,107kg)/58,340lb (26,463kg); max takeoff 100,000lb (45,360kg)/107,000lb (48,535kg); max landing 88,200lb (40,007kg); max payload 23,490lb (10,655kg)/22,950lb (10,410kg).

**Accommodation:** DC-6 - typically 52-58 first class passengers four abreast or 74 economy class; maximum 85 in high density layout; upper and lower berths for 26-39 passengers available in early versions. Baggage/freight capacity 373cu ft (10.5m$^3$) in two underfloor holds plus 91cu ft (2.6m$^3$) in forward cabin compartment.

DC-6A - total cargo volume 5,000cu ft (141.6m$^3$) comprising 4,433cu ft (125.5m$^3$) in cabin and 567cu ft (16.1m$^3$) in two underfloor holds.

DC-6B - typically 60-66 first class passengers in Domestic version or 54 in Overwater models; 82 economy class passengers or 92-102 in later high density configurations. Baggage/freight capacity 509cu ft (14.4m$^3$) in two underfloor holds.

**Performance:** DC-6 - max speed 307kt (568km/h) at 19,600ft; max cruise 274kt (507km/h) at 20,000ft; economical cruise 234kt (433km/h); initial climb 1,070ft (326m)/min; engine out climb 490ft (149m)/min; takeoff distance to 50ft 5,150ft (1,570m); operational ceiling 20,000ft; max payload range (no reserves) 2,442nm (4,523km); max range (no reserves) 3,300-3,700nm (6,112-6,855 km).

DC-6A - max speed 311kt (576km/h) at 18,100ft; cruising speed 270kt (500km/h) at 20,000ft; initial climb 1,120ft (341m)/min; engine out climb 530ft (161m)/min; takeoff distance to 50ft 6,150ft (1,875m); max payload range (no reserves) 2,540nm (4,705km); max range (no reserves) 3,334-4,242nm (6,175-7,857km).

DC-6B Domestic - max speed 311kt (576km/h) at 18,100ft; cruising speed 270kt (500km/h) at 20,000ft; initial climb 1,120ft (341m)/min; engine out climb 530ft (161m)/min; takeoff distance to 50ft 6,150ft (1,875m); operational ceiling 25,000ft; max payload range (no reserves) 2,610nm (4,835km); max range (no reserves) 3,953nm (7,323km).

DC-6B Overwater - as for Domestic except initial climb 1,080ft ((329m)/min; engine out climb 520ft (158m)/min; max range (no reserves) 4,325nm (8,010km).

# Military Sixes

The USAF received 101 C-118As between 1952 and 1956 based on the DC-6A Liftmaster. Resplendent in VIP colour scheme is C-118A 53-3240 (c/n 44611/628), delivered in December 1954 and photographed 11 years later at Sydney during a visit to Australia.

Of the 704 DC-6s of all models built between 1946 and 1958, 170 or 24 per cent of them were originally delivered to military customers: 103 for the US Air Force, 65 for the US Navy and two for the Belgian Air Force. Many second hand DC-6s were subsequently sold to military operators (see table below) - as were a handful of DC-7s - although no military versions of the latter were built from new.

Although the DC-6 and its developments are best known as commercial airliners, it must be remembered that the original project was instigated during World War II as an improved and more capable version of the DC-4/C-54 Skymaster then in widespread service with the United States Army Air Force.

As detailed in the previous chapter, the original prototype was built to a USAAF requirement as part of a government funded project (the 'Skymaster Improvement Program') which envisaged several variations on the basic design. The end of World War II and the massive reductions in aircraft procurement which resulted meant the requirement for such an aircraft disappeared - at least temporarily - leaving Douglas with the opportunity to develop the concept for the post war commercial market as the DC-6.

The military DC-6 versions were as follows:

**XC-112:** The original 1944 proposal for an 'improved C-54' combining that aircraft's unpressurised fuselage with more powerful 2,100hp (1,566kW) Pratt & Whitney R-2800C Double Wasp 18-cylinder radials in place of the C-54's 1,450hp (1,081kW) R-2000 Twin Wasp 14-cylinder radials. This project was dropped in favour of the stretched XC-112A concept.

**XC-112A:** In effect the prototype for the DC-6 series, the XC-112A differed from the earlier XC-112 design in having a 6ft 9in (2.06m) longer fuselage which increased standard seating capacity from 44 to 52 passengers four abreast. Powerplants were 2,100hp (1,566kW) R-2800-34s (the military designation), weights were increased and systems improved. A significant improvement was the incorporation of cabin pressurisation.

The sole XC-112A (c/n 36326) was allocated the USAAF serial 45-0873 and recorded its first flight on 15 February 1946. It was delivered to the USAAF on 22 June 1946 and subsequently redesignated YC-112A. Purchased by a commercial operator in 1955 it was converted to civil DC-6 standards the following year and enjoyed a lengthy career before being destroyed in a 1976 accident.

**YC-112A:** The XC-112A redesignated, the 'Y' prefix indicating 'evaluation'.

**XC-114:** One of the design concepts explored when the project was being

developed, the XC-114 was to have been powered by four Allison V-1710 vee-12 liquid cooled engines in place of the Pratt & Whitney R-2800 radials. It was cancelled in December 1945 before being built.

**XC-115:** Similar to the XC-114 but powered by Rolls-Royce Merlin vee-12 engines. Not built.

**XC-116:** Another variation of the basic design examined but cancelled in late 1945, the XC-116 was to have been powered by four General Electric TG-100 turboprops but they were unavailable.

**C-118:** The first DC-6 variant to enter regular military service, the sole C-118 (later VC-118), USAF serial 46-0505 (c/n 42881), was the 29th DC-6 off the production line and originally intended for American Airlines. The airline

**Spit and polish. C-118A 53-3240 was donated to the Pima Air Museum, Arizona for preservation in November 1978 where it remains in immaculate condition.**

USAF C-118A 51-3829 (c/n 43576/275) in Military Airlift Command colours in 1966, this organisation replacing the Military Air Transport Service (MATS). The 'O' prefix to the abbreviated serial number on the tail was a short-lived system used to indicate an aircraft which was more than 10 years old. (opposite)

sacrificed one of its delivery positions in order that the C-118 could be delivered for use as a presidential transport for Harry Truman.

Configured with 25 seats and 12 bunks, the aircraft was mechanically similar to a standard DC-6 and delivered on 1 July 1947, named *The Independence* after Truman's home town in Missouri. The VC-118 replaced VC-54C 41-107451 *Sacred Cow* in presidential service.

As an interesting sidelight, it was thought the VC-118 would have only a relatively short life as President Truman's main means of air transport. Lockheed VC-121B Constellation *Dewdrop* (48-0608) was delivered to the USAF in November 1948 in anticipation of Thomas Dewey defeating Harry Truman in that year's presidential election. Truman unexpectedly won the election and decided to retain *The Independence*, the VC-121B instead being used by other high ranking US Government and Air Force officials. The Constellation would have to wait until 1952 before becoming a presidential transport when VC-121A *Columbine II* 48-0610 was used by Dwight Eisenhower.

*The Independence* meanwhile remained as the presidential aircraft until then and was subsequently used as a general VIP transport before being retired and donated to the Smithsonian Institute for preservation in 1966.

**C-118A:** The USAF's C-118A (and R6D-1 for the USN) was the only DC-6 variant to achieve quantity production for the military and was fundamentally a military version of the DC-6A Liftmaster commercial freighter which had first flown in September 1949.

The C-118A shared the DC-6A's features including the stretched fuselage, two large freight doors fore and aft of the wing on the port side fuselage, freight loading system, floor tie downs and mechanical specification. Differences were confined to military-specific equipment and internal arrangements. Although primarily a cargo transport capable of carrying a payload of up to 27,000lb (12,247kg), the aircraft could be reconfigured to accommodate up to 76 passengers in rearwards facing seats or 60 casualty litters. Volumetric capacity was 4,433cu ft (125.5m$^3$) in the main cabin plus another 567cu ft (16.0m$^3$) in two underfloor holds.

Powerplants were four 2,500hp (1,864kW) with water-methanol injection R-2800-52W Double Wasps, the military equivalent of the DC-6A's R-2800-CB17. The C-118A's maximum allowable takeoff weight was 112,000lb (50,803kg) when operated as a freighter, 5,000lb (2,268kg) greater than the DC-6A.

Performance was similar to the DC-6A, figures including a cruising speed of 267kt (494km/h) at 22,400ft, initial climb rate of 1,120ft (341m)/min, and normal range of 3,334nm (6,175km).

The USAF began receiving its C-118As after the US Navy's R6D-1s, the

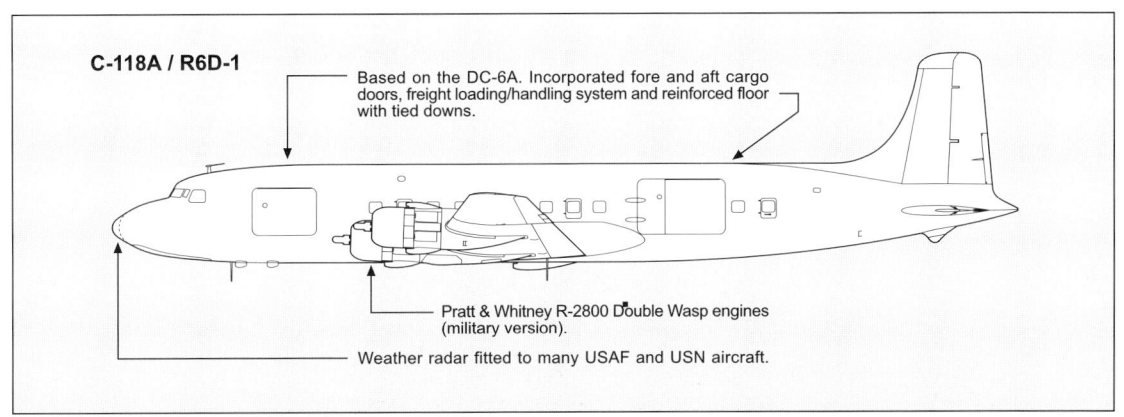

The US Navy received 65 DC-6As as the R6D-1 (later C-118B) from November 1951. BuAer 128427 (c/n 43210/206) was an R6D-1Z (VC-118B) VIP transport which also served with the US Marine Corps before it was put into storage in 1982. This shot was taken in October 1964.

first of 101 examples (51-3818, c/n 43565, line no 243) delivered on 16 July 1952, eight months after the first R6D-1 had been handed over. The last C-118A (53-3305, c/n 44676/644) was delivered on 10 January 1956, this aircraft becoming the personal transport of General Emmet O'Donnell, Commander-in-Chief of the Pacific Air Forces. A further 38 USN R6D-1s were transferred to the USAF in 1958, redesignated C-118A and allocated USAF serial numbers.

The C-118A was used mainly by the Military Air Transport Service's (MATS) Atlantic and Pacific Divisions on strategic transport duties around the world plus by the Headquarters of major USAF Commands. Later in their careers and after being retired from the longer haul MATS routes as more modern types entered service, many were used for shorter range medical evacuation (CASEVAC) flights Two were converted to VC-118A staff and VIP transports. One aircraft (51-3822) gained some unwanted fame in July 1952 when it was shot down by a Soviet fighter while flying over Armenia.

The USAF retired the bulk of its C-118A fleet in 1974-75, many of them subsequently being sold to civil operators to start second careers as commercial freighters. About 15 were formally redesignated as DC-6As while a dozen or so were transferred to the US Navy for three or four years' additional service before being disposed of.

**VC-118A:** Two C-118As (53-3229 and 53-3273) converted to VIP transports in 1964.

**C-118B:** September 1962 redesignation of R6D-1, as part of the new policy of aligning US military aircraft designations under the USAF system.

**VC-118B:** 1962 redesignation of one R6D-1Z VIP transport.

**R6D-1:** The US Navy version of the C-118A and the first military version of the DC-6 to be ordered in quantity. Similar in all major respects to the USAF's aircraft, the first R6D-1 (BuAer 128428, c/n 43401/207) was delivered on 16 November 1951 and the 65th and last (BuAer 131620, c/n 43723/377) on 20 August 1953. Three were converted to R6D-1Z VIP transports.

The Navy's R6D-1s served as part of the MATS system and with Fleet Logistic Air Wings and Naval Air Transport squadrons. Thirty-eight were transferred to the USAF in 1958 and redesignated C-118A (with new serial numbers) when that service was allocated the primary air transport responsibilities for the US military, these continuing to fly MATS operations in USAF colours but with Navy crews. Another five were also transferred to the US Marine Corps.

The remaining R6D-1s were redesignated as C-118Bs in 1962 and about 12 C-118As were transferred to the USN upon their retirement from USAF service in 1974-75. Other former US Navy R6D-1/C-118Bs also found their way back into service with their original operator. Most of the survivors had been retired by 1978-79, some of them then sold to commercial carriers.

**R6D-1Z:** Three R6D-1s (BuAer 128423, 128427 and 128433) converted to VIP transports. BuAer 128427 later redesignated VC-118B.

### The MATS System

The importance of airlift capability was continually and amply demonstrated during World War II, with the US Army Air Force contributing the lion's share of Allied air transport capacity during the conflict. By the end of hostilities in 1945, the USAAF's Air Transport Command (ATC) had 3,705 aircraft and more than 300,000 personnel (including contracted civilians) on its books. The US Navy also contributed a smaller but still considerable transport capability, the Naval Air Transport Service (NATS) operating a fleet of 431 aircraft by August 1945.

With the establishment of the independent US Air Force in September 1947 came a reorganisation of the service's structure, partly to meet new challenges but also due to the substantial reduction in strength following the end of the war. New conflicts over the next few years - notably in Korea - would see the USAF's strength built up again and in the interim the importance of airlift capability was recognised.

On 1 June 1948, Air Transport Command and the Naval Air Transport Service were consolidated to create the Military Air Transport Service (MATS) to operate a global air transport system for the Department of Defense and other US Government agencies. MATS also provided air communications, weather, rescue, photographic/charting and flight information services. USAF and USN transport aircraft and crews continued to carry their separate identities but worked together on a co-operative basis.

The basis premise of MATS was an integrated global air transport system for the US military (basically a trans-ocean, inter-theatre carrier), capable of moving personnel, equipment, mail and freight almost anywhere in the world on a routine basis. The ability of MATS to deal with an extraordinary situation was tested immediately after its formation in the Berlin Airlift of June 1948 to September 1949.

In wartime, the MATS fleet would be expanded by calling on the commercial transports which were part of the Civil Reserve Air Fleet (CRAF). The CRAF programme involved the modification of designated aircraft from the airlines so as to enable a quick changeover to war service. These modifications included the incorporation of the necessary wiring and hardware

**C-118A 53-3251 (c/n 446221/556) enjoyed a 20 year career with the USAF before being retired to storage in 1975. It was sold for scrap seven years later and broken up.**

to allow the fast installation of the communications and navigation equipment necessary for military operations. By 1957 about 300 four engined transports were available from this source.

In many ways, MATS developed into the world's largest airline, operating both scheduled and *ad hoc* services all over the world. By 1957 its route network covered 115,000 miles (185,000km) flying to some 60 ports in the mainland USA, Canada, the Caribbean, Central and South America, Greenland, Iceland, the Azores, Spain, Germany, Britain, North Africa, Egypt, Saudi Arabia, India, Thailand, South Vietnam, Okinawa, Japan, the Philippines, Hawaii and the Pacific Islands including Guam, Midway, Wake and Iwo Jima.

The initial MATS fleet in June 1948 comprised 824 aircraft, mainly Douglas C-54 Skymasters and C-47s. By early 1957 the fleet had grown to 1,435 aircraft including 610 four engined transports: C-54s, Boeing C-97s, Douglas C-118s (Navy R6D), Lockheed C-121s (Navy R7V) and Douglas C-124 Globemasters. More modern types such as the Douglas C-133 Cargomaster and C-130 Hercules turboprops would shortly be part of the MATS inventory.

MATS remained in existence until the mid 1960s when it was replaced by the reorganised Military Airlift Command (MAC). By then, new military transport types such as the Lockheed C-141 Starlifter and C-5 Galaxy were part of the equation, the former just entering service and the latter under development for service entry in late 1969.

**DC-6AB FAS301 (c/n 45078/722) was the sole example of the type to serve with the El Salvador Air Force, delivered in 1976. It was originally built as a DC-6B for Canadian Pacific Airlines in 1956 which leased it out to several operators including Air Liban and Cunard Eagle.**

**The Royal New Zealand Air Force operated three DC-6s from May 1961, all of them previously owned by Australia's British Commonwealth Pacific Airways and New Zealand's Tasman Empire Airways Ltd (TEAL). NZ3631 (c/n 43126/132) was originally delivered to BCPA in November 1948.**

The South Vietnam Air Force operated a single DC-6B between 1966 and 1975, but Air Vietnam aircraft were sometimes used for government and military purposes. DC-6B XV-NUC (c/n 44699/621) was one of them and is shown here visiting Australia during the Vietnam War. The aircraft was originally Northwest Orient's N570.

Former USAF C-118A 53-3294 (c/n 44665/632) had several owners after it was retired from military service in 1974. The International Shoe Machine Corp operated it 1978-86 as N43872.

### C-118A and R6D-1 Annual Deliveries

| Year | C-118A | R6D-1 | Total |
|---|---|---|---|
| 1951 | - | 3 | 3 |
| 1952 | 17 | 17 | 34 |
| 1953 | 1 | 45 | 46 |
| 1954 | 20 | - | 20 |
| 1955 | 61 | - | 61 |
| 1956 | 2 | - | 2 |
| Totals | 101 | 65 | 166 |

### Other Military Operators

Apart from the USA, the air forces of 22 other nations between them operated some 80 DC-6 variants while four countries flew seven DC-7s. All of these were purchased second hand with the exception of two of Belgium's DC-6As which were delivered new in 1958. No new DC-7s were sold to military operators.

Some were acquired by unconventional means: the Colombian Air Force DC-6s and DC-7s were seized by the Colombian Government after it was discovered they were being used for drug trafficking.

The following table lists all non US military DC-6s and DC-7s individually, noting the country, model, national serial number, constructor's number/line number, period of service and notes.

| Country | Serial | Model | C/n & l/no | Dates | Notes |
|---|---|---|---|---|---|
| Argentina | T-51 | DC-6 | 43030/124 | 1966-73 | ex Aerolineas Argentinas |
| | T-52 | DC-6 | 43032/128 | 1966-73 | ex Aerolineas Argentinas |
| | T-53 | DC-6 | 43033/134 | 1966-73 | ex Aerolineas Argentinas |
| | TC-54 | DC-6A/B | 44102/388 | 1967-73 | ex Pan Am |
| | TC-55 | DC-6A/B | 44114/453 | 1967-68 | ex Pan Am |
| Belgium | KY-1 | DC-6A | 45458/986 | 1958-77 | delivered new |
| | KY-2 | DC-6A | 45518/998 | 1958-77 | delivered new |
| | KY-3 | DC-6A | 44420/479 | 1960-77 | ex Sabena |
| | KY-4 | DC-6A | 44421/489 | 1960-77 | ex Sabena |
| Bolivia | TAM-63 | DC-6B | 43543/210 | 1974-80 | ex Pan Am |
| Brazil | 2412 | DC-6B | 44166/416 | 1968-75 | ex SAS/Varig |
| | 2413 | DC-6B | 43745/296 | 1968-73 | ex SAS/Varig |
| | 2414 | DC-6B | 43746/297 | 1968-71 | ex SAS/Varig |
| | 2415 | DC-6B | 43822/291 | 1968-75 | ex Western/Northwest/Varig |
| | 2416 | DC-6B | 43824/299 | 1968-75 | ex Western/Northwest/Varig |
| Chile | FAC 985 | DC-6A/B | 45179/865 | 1966-82 | ex Western |
| | FAC 986 | DC-6A/B | 45177/859 | 1966-82 | ex Western |
| | FAC 987 | DC-6A/B | 43522/229 | 1967-82 | ex Pan Am |
| | FAC 988 | DC-6A/B | 44057/354 | 1967-82 | ex American/JAL |
| | FAC 989 | DC-6B | 45534/1012 | 1973-83 | ex Western/LAN Chile |
| | FAC 990 | DC-6B | 45536/1021 | 1973-80 | ex Western/LAN Chile |
| Colombia | FAC 902 | DC-6B | 45067/709 | 1981- | ex Western/JAL etc, impounded by Colombian Govt |
| | FAC 909 | DC-6A | 43841/386 | 1983- | ex American etc, impounded by Colombian Govt |
| | FAC 921 | DC-7BF | 44923/671 | 1981- | ex American etc, impounded by Colombian Govt |
| | FAC 923 | DC-7C | 45111/727 | 1981- | ex BOAC/Saturn, impounded by Colombian Govt |
| Ecuador | FAE43266 | DC-6BF | 43266/182 | 1964-72 | ex American |
| | FAE43564 | DC-6B | 43564/212 | 1965-74 | ex American |
| | FAE44691 | DC-6B | 44691/552 | 1971-78 | ex LAN Chile |
| | FAE45063 | DC-6B | 45063/678 | 1971-78 | ex Western/Braniff |
| | FAE45133 | DC-6B | 45133/807 | 1975-83 | ex United |
| | FAE45535 | DC-6B | 45535/1018 | 1971-86 | ex Western/LAN Chile |
| El Salvador | FAS301 | DC-6A/B | 45078/722 | 1976- | ex Canadian Pacific |
| France | 43748 | DC-6B | 43748/314 | 1961-68 | ex SAS |
| | 82-PU | DC-6A | 43818/338 | 1967-77 | ex Slick/UAT |
| | 82-PV | DC-6A | 43819/348 | 1967-78 | ex Slick/UAT |
| | 64-PI | DC-6B | 43834/379 | 1966-77 | ex TAI/UTA |
| | 64-PJ | DC-6A/B | 44697/598 | 1965-78 | ex TAI/UTA |
| | 82-PZ | DC-6A/B | 45107/749 | 1962-77 | ex Trans American |
| | 82-PW | DC-6A | 45226/885 | 1966-78 | ex Air Liban/Air France |
| | 82-PY | DC-6B | 45108/770 | 1962-77 | ex Trans American |
| | 45109 | DC-6B | 45109/786 | 1974-80 | ex Trans American/Air France |
| | 82-PW | DC-6A | 45226/885 | 1966-78 | ex Air Liban/Air France |
| | 64-PK | DC-6A/B | 45472/972 | 1962-77 | ex Trans American |
| | 64-PL | DC-6A/B | 45473/978 | 1962-77 | ex Trans American |
| | 82-PX | DC-6C | 45481/991 | 1966-69 | ex Air Liban/Air France |
| | 85-CA | DC-7C | 45061/733 | 1963-70 | ex Swissair/SAS |
| | 85-CB | DC-7C | 45367/918 | 1964-78 | ex TAI |
| | 85-CC | DC-7C | 45446/927 | 1964-74 | ex TAI |

| Country | Serial | Model | C/n & l/no | Dates | Notes |
|---|---|---|---|---|---|
| W Germany | 13+01 | DC-6A/B | 43828/349 | 1965-69 | ex Sabena |
| | 13+02 | DC-6A/B | 44175/435 | 1965-69 | ex Sabena |
| | 13+03 | DC-6B | 45065/693 | 1962-69 | ex Western |
| | 13+04 | DC-6B | 45066/696 | 1962-69 | ex Western |
| Guatemala | 926 | DC-6B/F | 45539/1010 | 1973- | ex Olympic |
| Honduras | 800 | C-118A | 44642/586 | 1977- | ex USAF |
| Italy | MM61900 | DC-6 | 43152/161 | 1963-79 | ex Alitalia |
| | MM61910 | DC-6B | 44913/663 | 1964-68 | ex Alitalia |
| | MM61922 | DC-6 | 43216/165 | 1965-81 | ex Alitalia |
| | MM61923 | DC-6 | 43217/166 | 1966-80 | ex Alitalia |
| | MM61964 | DC-6B | 44253/448 | 1969-75 | ex Alitalia |
| | MM61965 | DC-6B | 44251/420 | 1970-78 | ex Alitalia |
| | MM61987 | DC-6B | 44252/442 | 1970-74 | ex Alitalia |
| | MM61987 | DC-6B | 44417/473 | 1970-75 | ex Alitalia |
| Mexico | TP-203 | DC-6 | 43129/106 | 1964-78 | ex SAS/Mexicana |
| | ETP-10001 | DC-6A/B | 44059/366 | 1968-72 | ex American |
| | ETP-10003 | DC-6 | 43134/117 | 1966-75 | ex SAS/Mexicana |
| | ETP-10017 | DC-6A | 43819/348 | 1983- | ex Slick/UTA/ French AF |
| | ETP-10018 | DC-6A | 44226/885 | 1979- | ex Air Liban/Air France/ French AF |
| | ETP-10103 | DC-7B | 45407/899 | 1964-70 | ex American |
| New Zealand | NZ3631 | DC-6 | 43126/132 | 1961-68 | ex BCPA/TEAL |
| | NZ3632 | DC-6 | 43127/133 | 1961-64 | ex BCPA/TEAL |
| | NZ3633 | DC-6 | 43128/135 | 1961-64 | ex BCPA/TEAL |
| Panama | FAP401 | DC-6B | 43521/228 | 1970-75 | ex Pan Am etc |
| Paraguay | 4001 | DC-6B | 43822/291 | 1975- | from Brazil AF |
| | 4002 | DC-6B | 43824/299 | 1975- | from Brazil AF |
| | 4003 | DC-6B | 44166/416 | 1975- | from Brazil AF |
| Portugal | 6701 | DC-6A/B | 44107/411 | 1961-71 | ex Pan Am |
| | 6703 | DC-6A | 44258/467 | 1961-76 | ex Pan Am |
| | 6704 | DC-6A | 43297/213 | 1960-78 | ex Slick/Pan Am |
| | 6705 | DC-6B | 44115/454 | 1961-78 | ex Pan Am |
| | 6706 | DC-6B | 44116/459 | 1961-78 | ex Pan Am |
| | 6707 | DC-6B | 43533/264 | 1961-78 | ex Pan Am |
| | 6708 | DC-6B | 43534/265 | 1961-78 | ex Pan Am |
| | 6709 | DC-6B | 43535/278 | 1961-76 | ex Pan Am |
| | 6710 | DC-6B | 43529/260 | 1961-76 | ex Pan Am |
| Rhodesia | 7230 | DC-7CF | 45188/837 | 1979-80 | leased from Affretair, ex KLM |
| Saudi Arabia | SA-R-6 | DC-6B | 44167/426 | 1960-64 | ex SAS, Royal Family use |
| Sth Vietnam | 111 | DC-6B | 44111/430 | 1966-75 | ex Pan Am, seized by Hang Khong Vietnam, operated 1975-80 |
| Yugoslavia | 7451 | DC-6B | 45563/1034 | 1961-75 | ex JAT |
| | 7452 | DC-6B | 45564/1040 | 1966-75 | ex JAT, last DC-6 |
| Zambia | GBM 110 | DC-6B | 45563/1034 | 1975- | from Yugoslav AF |
| | GBM 112 | DC-6B | 45564/1040 | 1975- | from Yugoslav AF |

# Douglas DC-7

The DC-7 as we now know it - the final expression of the line which began with the DC-4 and continued through the DC-6 models - was not the first Douglas aircraft to carry that designation. The original DC-7 was intended to be a civil version of the C-74 Globemaster I long range heavy military transport developed during World War II for the USAAF.

A very big aircraft for its time (nearly 25 per cent larger in wing span and length than a B-29 Superfortress) the Globemaster was powered by four 3,500hp (2,610kW) Pratt & Whitney R-4360 Wasp Major 28-cylinder radials. Normal maximum takeoff weight was 145,000lb (65,772kg) - twice that of a DC-4 - and it was capable of carrying a payload of up to 55,500lb (25,175kg) or 125 equipped troops. A novel feature was separate cockpits side-by-side under individual canopies but a more conventional arrangement was soon adopted.

The first C-74 flew in October 1945, two months after the Pacific War had ended. Faced with substantial costs and the fact that the C-74 was no longer really needed, the USAAF cancelled most of its order and only 14 were built.

Pan American had expressed an interest in a civil version for post war use as a luxury 'clipper' for services from the USA to Latin America. The airline envisaged the aircraft carrying 108 passengers in spacious comfort in the manner of its pre war flying boats and in October 1944 placed a provisional order for 26. As Douglas already had the DC-6 designation allocated through the Skymaster Improvement Program it was then working on, the next number in the Douglas Commercial sequence was applied to the civil C-74 - DC-7.

Unfortunately for Pan American the concept of gracious (and space wasting) air travel was not compatible with the post war world and the C-74/DC-7 project was cancelled in 1947.

### Sixes and Sevens

The real DC-7's origins can be found in early 1951 as a result of pressure on the manufacturers from US domestic airlines to produce an airliner

**The DC-7 was developed to provide US domestic carriers with an aircraft capable of performing non stop coast-to-coast flights in either direction. United was the biggest customer, taking delivery of 57 from April 1954. DC-7 N6322C *Mainliner Philadelphia* (c/n 44286/530) is photographed over Honolulu's Waikiki Beach.**

which was capable of performing non stop coast-to-coast flights across the country in either direction. Most of the pressure was coming from American Airlines' Cyrus Smith who had a close relationship with Douglas and was mainly responsible for the project going ahead, just as he had been with the DC-3 15 years earlier.

Market pressure was also coming from Lockheed, which had launched the stretched L.1049 Super Constellation in 1950 with orders from Eastern and TWA, with service entry scheduled for late 1951. An improved, longer range version - the L.1049C - was also planned and would enter service in 1953, around the same time as the improved DC-6 should it go ahead.

Douglas was reluctant to commit to what emerged as the DC-7 because the strong selling DC-6B was being delivered from 1951 and would begin service with American and United in April. There was concern that a new model might take sales away from the DC-6B and that its development costs might reduce company profits. Douglas had a similar attitude towards the DC-3 and its possible effect on the DC-2 when Cyrus Smith pushed for its development in 1935. It did, but more than compensated!

The company was also hesitant about further developing the piston engined airliner concept because the turboprop was starting to look viable as a powerplant for commercial aircraft and the de Havilland Comet jet was flying and within a year of entering service.

Smith persisted, and in December 1951 Douglas agreed to start development of the DC-7, basing it around the new Wright R-3350 Turbo Compound 18-cylinder radial. American Airlines responded positively, immediately ordering 25 at a price of $US1.6 million each, a substantial $US480,000 (43 per cent) more than the DC-6B's list price. Subsequent customers were quoted a unit price of $US1.76 million for the DC-7.

Offering 30 per cent more power than the DC-6's Pratt & Whitney R-2800 Double Wasp, the Turbo Compound was a new version of the R-3350 Cyclone which had powered the Boeing B-29 Superfortress bomber and early versions of the Lockheed Constellation. It was also the selected powerplant for the L.1049C and later Constellation models.

While the earlier R-3350s were conventionally supercharged by two-speed gear driven systems and produced up to 2,700hp (2,013kW), the Turbo Compound derived additional power from its pair of superchargers which were 'compounded' by three 'blow down' exhaust gas power recovery

**The DC-7C 'Seven Seas' represented the pinnacle of Douglas piston engined commercial transport design and was the first airliner capable of routinely flying the Atlantic east-west non stop against the wind. As such, it stole a march on the Lockheed opposition in the last years of the piston engined airliner. N70C (c/n 44872/653) was the first DC-7C, flying on 20 December 1955. It was later sold to Panair do Brasil.**

turbines mounted on the rear section of the crankcase. The exhaust pipes from six adjacent engine cylinders were connected to each turbine intake, the gasses from these feeding back to the engine and producing an extra 550hp (410kW).

The Turbo Compound retained the basic characteristics of earlier R-3350s: 18-cylinder two row radial, cylinder bore 6.125in (155mm), piston stroke 6.3125in (160mm), displacement 3,347cu in (54.9 litres), maximum revolutions 2,900rpm and the use of 115/145 octane fuel. Compression ratio was 6.7:1 and specific fuel consumption at cruise power 0.38lb/hp/hr, a 12 per cent improvement over the previous engine.

The DA-series engine used in the initial DC-7 and subsequent DC-7B produced 3,250hp (2,423kW) for takeoff at 2,900rpm, 2,650hp (1,976kW) at 6,500ft and 2,600rpm, and 2,450hp (1,827kW) at 17,900ft and 2,600rpm.

The advanced and complex Turbo Compound provided the necessary power for the DC-7 but at the cost of initial unreliability due mainly to problems with the power recovery turbines and associated systems. Three

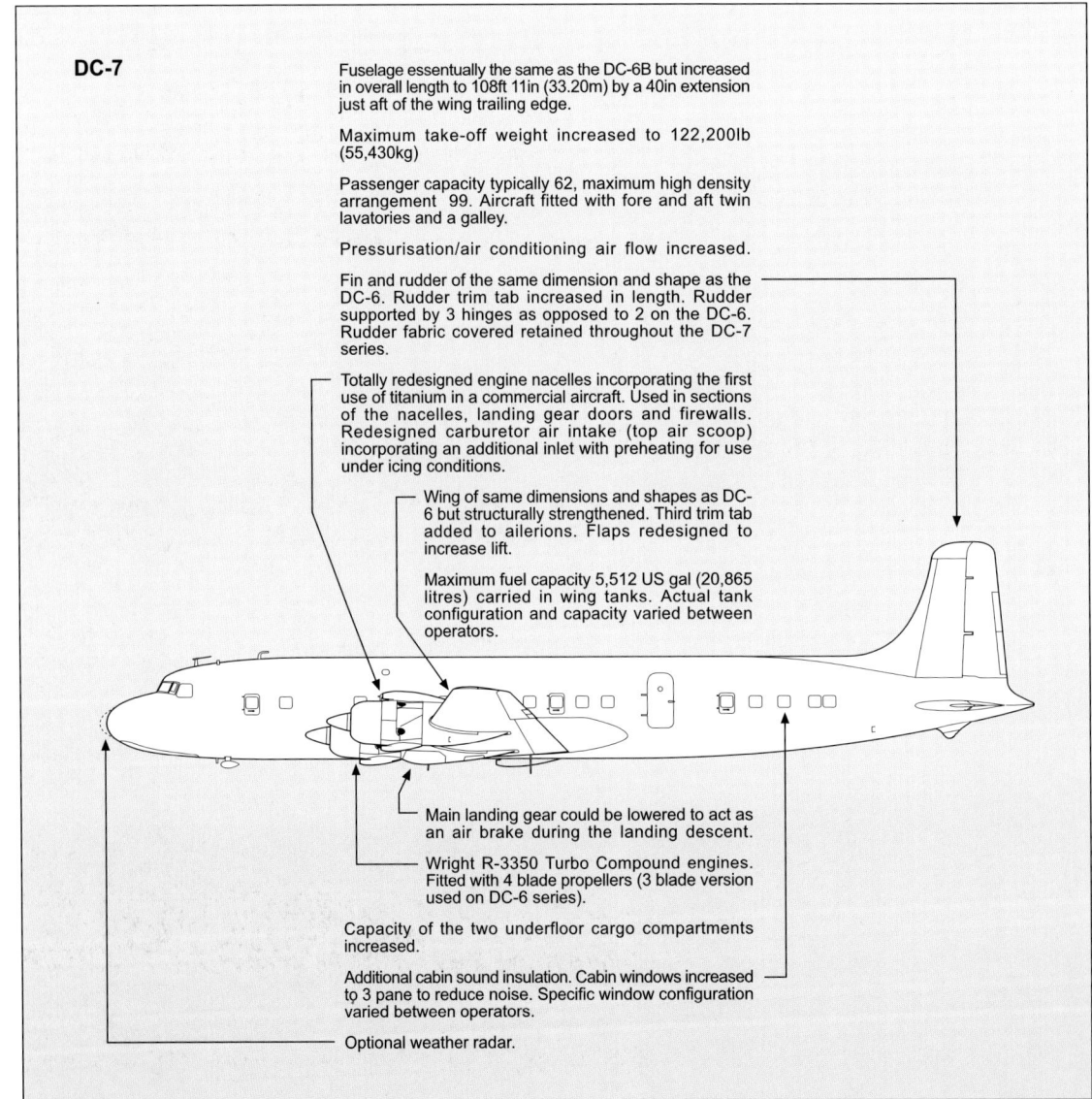

**DC-7**

Fuselage essentually the same as the DC-6B but increased in overall length to 108ft 11in (33.20m) by a 40in extension just aft of the wing trailing edge.

Maximum take-off weight increased to 122,200lb (55,430kg)

Passenger capacity typically 62, maximum high density arrangement 99. Aircraft fitted with fore and aft twin lavatories and a galley.

Pressurisation/air conditioning air flow increased.

Fin and rudder of the same dimension and shape as the DC-6. Rudder trim tab increased in length. Rudder supported by 3 hinges as opposed to 2 on the DC-6. Rudder fabric covered retained throughout the DC-7 series.

Totally redesigned engine nacelles incorporating the first use of titanium in a commercial aircraft. Used in sections of the nacelles, landing gear doors and firewalls. Redesigned carburetor air intake (top air scoop) incorporating an additional inlet with preheating for use under icing conditions.

Wing of same dimensions and shapes as DC-6 but structurally strengthened. Third trim tab added to ailerions. Flaps redesigned to increase lift.

Maximum fuel capacity 5,512 US gal (20,865 litres) carried in wing tanks. Actual tank configuration and capacity varied between operators.

Main landing gear could be lowered to act as an air brake during the landing descent.

Wright R-3350 Turbo Compound engines. Fitted with 4 blade propellers (3 blade version used on DC-6 series).

Capacity of the two underfloor cargo compartments increased.

Additional cabin sound insulation. Cabin windows increased to 3 pane to reduce noise. Specific window configuration varied between operators.

Optional weather radar.

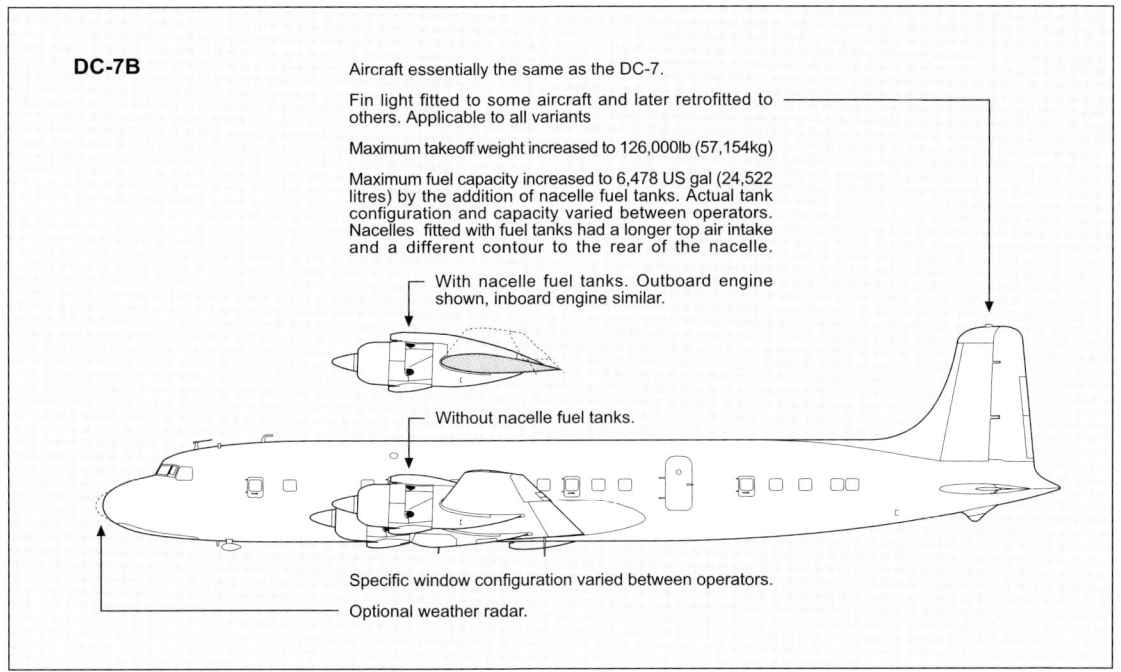

engined arrivals were common until most of the problems were sorted out in later versions of the engines.

Other changes incorporated in the DC-7 included the use of four (rather than three) bladed Hamilton Standard propellers, a 3ft 4in (1.01m) longer fuselage and a substantial 14 per cent increase in maximum takeoff weight to 122,200lb (55,430kg). The wing and empennage remained as before except for the wing strengthening required to handle the increased weights. The engine nacelles and engine mounting systems were redesigned to cope with the greater physical dimensions, weight and power of the R-3350.

The fuel capacity of 5,512 USgal (20,865 l) was the same as the highest option available on the DC-6B and thanks to the DC-7's payload-range capabilities was sufficient to allow those much desired non stop US east-west coast flights. Normal passenger capacity was 62 in a four abreast first class layout with later economy class and high density layouts allowing up to 99 to be carried.

A significant operational (and marketing) benefit the DC-7 offered was a cruising speed about 40 knots (74km/h) faster than the best the DC-6B could manage and faster than the similarly powered L.1049C Super Constellation. The Connie had superior range and was ordered mainly by international carriers whereas the original DC-7 was operated solely by US trunk carriers. The important L.1049C exception was Eastern Air Lines, which put its new Super Constellations into service in November 1953 on US trunk routes, the same month American Airlines introduced the DC-7.

Under the DC-7's skin there were many detail changes. A significant one was the first use in a commercial transport of light and heat resistant titanium in some areas such as the aft engine nacelles (where it offered some protection against fire), some frames and the undercarriage doors.

An attempt was made to reduce cabin noise by the installation of 1,200lb (544kg) of sound deadening material in the cabin wall between the internal lining and the skin, while the cabin windows received a third pane of glass which was free floating in rubber, this helping reduce not only noise but also vibration.

Otherwise, the DC-7 was similar to the DC-6B with minor changes such as beefing up the electrical system and simplifying and enlarging the engine oil system incorporated. One interesting innovation was the installation of alternate anti-icing carburettor intakes within the standard scoops mounted on top of the engine nacelles. The alternate intake could be selected for use in conditions conducive to icing and in normal operating conditions the standard intake was used.

Despite the company's initial concerns about the DC-7's financial viability, the aircraft went on to turn a nice profit for Douglas with 338 built in three versions. The DC-7 was produced on the same assembly line as the DC-6 at Santa Monica, the close relationship between the two aircraft further indicated by the manufacturer's line or 'fuselage' numbers which were shared between the two types.

**Pan American was the major driving force behind development of the long range DC-7C and ordered 26 for its international operations. N739PA *Clipper Flora Temple* (c/n 44881/692) was delivered in June 1956.**

### DC-7 Into Service

The first DC-7 (N301AA, c/n 44122, line number 350) *Flagship Texas* for American Airlines was flown on 18 May 1953 ahead of a six month certification programme which ended on 12 November. By then four DC-7s were flying and others were either being readied for delivery or nearing completion. *Flagship Texas* remained with Douglas until April 1954 when it was handed over to the airline after completing its test duties.

American Airlines received its first aircraft (N304AA *Flagship Illinois*, c/n 44125/390) on 10 October 1953. A second DC-7 joined the fleet three weeks later and both were used for training and proving flights before regular services began. By late December 1953 the airline had taken delivery of eight DC-7s and a further 12 would be in service by the end of the first quarter of 1954.

American inaugurated DC-7 services on 29 November 1953 on its daily New York-Los Angles service. The scheduled time for the journey was 8hr 45min (and just on eight hours for the return trip with a tailwind), both of these about two hours faster than the original DC-6 could manage thanks to there no longer being the need for a fuel stop and higher cruising speeds.

American eventually took delivery of 34 DC-7s, the last of them (N334AA, c/n 45106/738) *Flagship Vermont* in November 1956.

All of the 105 DC-7s built were sold to US domestic airlines, others being ordered by National Airlines (4, delivered from November 1953), United (57 from April 1954) and Delta (10 from February 1954). The last standard DC-7 was United's N6357C *Mainliner Salem* (c/n 45490 and the 1,000th of the DC-6/7 line) delivered in July 1958.

National launched DC-7 services on the New York-Miami route in competition with Eastern's new L.1049C Super Constellations, and Delta's first service was between Chicago and Florida. Delta contributed a piece of history to the DC-7 story on 1 April 1955 when it launched the type's first 'intercontinental' service to various ports in the Caribbean.

The DC-7 was more expensive to operate in terms of seat-mile costs than the DC-6B, while acquisition costs were also higher and the relatively poor reliability of the Turbo Compound compared to the dependable R-2800 was also a negative. This also effected resale values but overall the DC-7 was still able to make money for its operators and its combination of higher speed and improved payload-range performance bestowed operational advantages over the DC-6B.

One of United's DC-7s was involved in a very high profile accident. On 30 June 1956 N6324C *Mainliner Vancouver* and a TWA Super Constellation collided over the Grand Canyon with the loss of all aboard both aircraft. The accident prompted a shakeup of US air traffic control procedures when it was revealed that although controllers knew the two aircraft were at the same altitude and on converging tracks, the fact they were flying outside controlled airspace meant there was no legal obligation to inform the flight crews of the conflict in a 'see and be seen' situation.... so they didn't.

American Airlines began disposing of its DC-7 fleet as early as April 1959 when its first 25 aircraft were sold as a package deal to the Galco company for resale. Several found no buyers and were eventually scrapped for spares while 12 were leased by Overseas National Airlines.

Others went to the US Federal Aviation Administration, Standard Airways

**An impressive list of international carriers purchased the DC-7C for their long range operations including a couple who had previously been Lockheed customers. KLM was one which chose the DC-7C over the Lockheed Starliner, its PH-DSL *Baltic Sea* (c/n 45180/789) photographed at the time of delivery in April 1957.**

and Lebanese International Airways, mostly after having been in storage for several years. The FAA aircraft (ex N306AA, c/n 44127/402) was used to test the autoland system developed by Britain's Blind Landing Experimental Unit. American's other DC-7s were retired in 1962-63, followed by United's from 1963, National's from 1964 and Delta's from 1966. Six United aircraft were converted to freighters while still in the airline's service.

## DC-7A

The DC-7A designation was not used by Douglas which went straight from the DC-7 to DC-7B for marketing reasons when that model was introduced. The 'A' designation was kept in reserve in case a new production freighter version was developed (which it never was) in order to continue the theme established by the DC-6A Liftmaster. When United Airlines converted six of its DC-7s to freighters it gave them the unofficial designation DC-7A in acknowledgement of the precedent set by the DC-6A.

## DC-7B

The airlines' calls for more range inspired development of the DC-7B, as did the introduction to service of the L.1049C Super Constellation in August 1953, three months before the original DC-7 began operations. The L.1049C could travel about 360nm (666km) further than the DC-7 and Douglas once again found itself playing catch up in this area. The DC-7B matched the L.1049C's maximum range but Lockheed was not standing still, introducing the even longer legged L.1049G to service in January 1955, five months before the DC-7B.

Further, the L.1049G had superior range when carrying a heavy payload but the bottom line was that neither it nor the DC-7B were capable of non stop east-west crossings of the Atlantic most of the time.

Despite this, eight airlines purchased 112 DC-7Bs although it is perhaps ironic that most of these went to US domestic carriers who chose not to take advantage of the additional fuel capacity which was available to them.

The full customer list for the DC-7B was American (24), Continental (6), Delta (11), Eastern (50), National (4), Pan American (7), Panagra (6) and

SAS continued its association with Douglas airliners by taking delivery of 14 DC-7Cs, using them to pioneer true 'over the pole' services in February 1957. LN-MOF *Roald Viking* (c/n 45212/866) was delivered in September 1957.

BOAC ordered ten DC-7Cs as an interim measure due to service entry delays suffered by the airline's Bristol Britannia turboprops. G-AOIA (c/n 45111/727) was the first of them, delivered in October 1956.

South African Airways (4). Of these only 110 were delivered as one each for Continental and Eastern was lost before delivery. Continental's N8210H (c/n 45192/764) collided with a USAF Northrop F-89 Scorpion fighter over California in January 1957 and the Eastern's N846D (c/n 45452/967) crashed during a test flight in March 1958.

Douglas launched the DC-7B in April 1953 and Pan American placed the first order (for seven) the following December. The DC-7B retained the original DC-7's dimensions, powerplants, propellers and other major features but could have an additional 968 USgal (3,664 l) of fuel housed mainly in enlarged engine nacelle saddle tanks, an optional increased maximum takeoff weight of 126,000lb (57,154kg) and an improved flap operating system.

Of the 112 built, only the 11 for Pan American and South African Airways could be regarded as true DC-7Bs with all the new features incorporated. The remainder were DC-7/7B hybrids without the nacelle tanks and increased maximum weight, the additional range these improvements bestowed not needed on the US domestic services for which most of the aircraft were used.

The DC-7B's biggest order - 50 from Eastern Air Lines - was significant to the overall DC-7 programme. Eastern had previously been a dedicated user of Lockheed Constellations and ordered some 60 over the years. It had flown leased DC-6Bs for a time and its large contract for the $US1.9 million DC-7B was an unexpected and pleasant one for Douglas.

The first DC-7B (N70D, c/n 44435/486) flew in October 1954 and was subsequently delivered to Delta Air Lines as N4881C. Initial deliveries were to Pan American in June 1955 followed by Panagra and Eastern in the same month then Delta (December 1955), South African (February 1956), American (March 1956), Continental (March 1957) and National (October 1957).

Pan American operated the inaugural DC-7B service on 13 June 1955 on a New York-London flight, while the only other operator of 'true' DC-7Bs - South African Airways - introduced them on the 'Springbok Route' to London in April 1956.

The last DC-7B was N850D (c/n 45456/982) delivered to Eastern on 23 May 1958. The original owners had disposed of most of their fleets by 1965-66. Fourteen were subsequently converted to freighters.

## Battle for the Market

As has been noted several times in this book, the battle for market share between Douglas and Lockheed raged for more than a decade as they continually developed their DC-6/7 and Constellation designs. Much of this development revolved around the constant need for additional range and Douglas often found itself playing 'catch up' in this area as it strove to match the Constellation and meet the airlines' requirements.

An exception was right at the end of the piston engined airliner era when Douglas developed the DC-7C which was capable of crossing the Atlantic non stop in both directions, something which had previously been impossible when travelling east-west against the prevailing wind. In this case Lockheed was forced to react with the Starliner which entered service a nearly year after the DC-7C and suffered commercially as a result.

For comparison purposes, the following table presents the DC-6, DC-7, L.049/749 Constellation, L.1049 Super Constellation and L.1649A Starliner combatants (excluding dedicated freighter and military versions but including convertible variants) in chronological order of entering service, showing the date of service entry, the typical number of first class passengers carried in early configurations for overseas operations (Pax), no reserves range with the maximum available fuel capacity, and the quantity (Qty) of commercial versions built.

Note that the original DC-7 and L.1049 Super Constellation were ordered only by US carriers for use on domestic trunk routes.

Broken down, the figures reveal that Douglas sold a total of 469 DC-6 passenger models versus 206 Lockheed Constellations; and 338 DC-7s versus 303 commercial Super Constellations and Starliners.

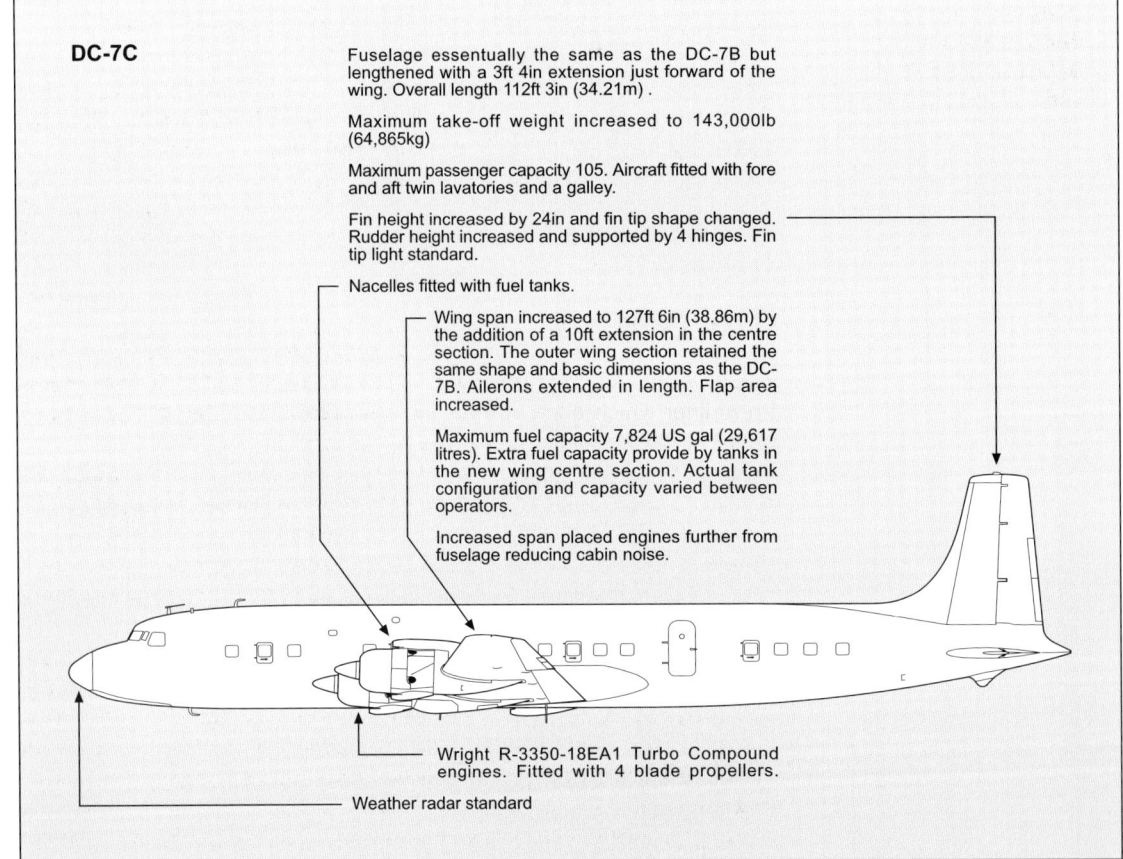

**DC-7C**

Fuselage essentually the same as the DC-7B but lengthened with a 3ft 4in extension just forward of the wing. Overall length 112ft 3in (34.21m).

Maximum take-off weight increased to 143,000lb (64,865kg)

Maximum passenger capacity 105. Aircraft fitted with fore and aft twin lavatories and a galley.

Fin height increased by 24in and fin tip shape changed. Rudder height increased and supported by 4 hinges. Fin tip light standard.

Nacelles fitted with fuel tanks.

Wing span increased to 127ft 6in (38.86m) by the addition of a 10ft extension in the centre section. The outer wing section retained the same shape and basic dimensions as the DC-7B. Ailerons extended in length. Flap area increased.

Maximum fuel capacity 7,824 US gal (29,617 litres). Extra fuel capacity provide by tanks in the new wing centre section. Actual tank configuration and capacity varied between operators.

Increased span placed engines further from fuselage reducing cabin noise.

Wright R-3350-18EA1 Turbo Compound engines. Fitted with 4 blade propellers.

Weather radar standard

JA6301 *City of San Francisco* (c/n 45468/910) was the first of JAL's four DC-7Cs and was delivered in December 1957. By then both the DC-7 and DC-6 were entering their final year of production.

| Type | In Service | Pax | Maximum Range | Qty |
|---|---|---|---|---|
| L.049 | Feb 1946 | 48 | 3,200nm (5,925km) | 73 |
| L.649/A | March 1947 | 48 | 3,740nm (6,430km) | 20 |
| 749/A | March 1947 | 48 | 4,210nm (7,798km) | 113 |
| DC-6 | April 1947 | 52 | 3,700nm (6,855km) | 174 |
| DC-6B/C | April 1951 | 60 | 4,325nm (8,010km) | 295 |
| L.1049 | Dec 1951 | 69 | 2,268nm (4,200km)* | 24 |
| L.1049C/D/E | Aug 1953 | 69 | 4,136nm (7,660km) | 78 |
| DC-7 | Nov 1953 | 62 | 3,770nm (6,983km) | 105 |
| L.1049G/H | Jan 1955 | 69 | 4,562nm (8,450km) | 157 |
| DC-7B | June 1955 | 62 | 4,275nm (7,918km) | 112 |
| DC-7C | June 1956 | 62 | 4,900nm (9,076km) | 121 |
| L.1649A | May 1957 | 64 | 5,370nm (9,945km) | 44 |

* maximum payload range

### DC-7C Seven Seas

The ultimate development of the Douglas piston engined family, the DC-7C was conceived to meet the needs of Pan American and others who wanted an airliner which once and for all was capable of flying the Atlantic non stop in both directions regardless of the prevailing wind.

The resulting DC-7C or 'Seven Seas' as it became known represented - along with the Lockheed Starliner - the pinnacle of piston engined airliner development, filling the gap for a few years until the Boeing 707 and Douglas DC-8 jets came into service. The 'Seven Seas' play of words on the designation appropriately reflected its role as a long range, intercontinental airliner.

For once, the DC-7C gave Douglas a clear lead over its Lockheed rival in the 'top end' airliner marketplace, entering service in June 1956, nearly a year ahead of the Starliner. This was a rewinged, heavier and more powerful variant of the Super Constellation and although its ultimate range was greater than the DC-7C's, it was too late and only 44 were built for just three airlines.

By comparison, Douglas manufactured 121 DC-7Cs for 13 operators,

some of which had previously been loyal Lockheed customers but found themselves with little choice but to switch to the Douglas product in order to remain competitive. It was also discovered that the DC-7C's operating economics were notably superior to the Starliner's.

The airlines which took delivery of DC-7Cs direct from the manufacturer were Alitalia (6), BOAC (10 to cover lengthy delays with the Bristol Britannia turboprop), Braniff (7), JAL (4), KLM (15), Mexicana (3), Northwest Orient (14), Panair do Brasil (4 including the prototype), Pan American (26), Sabena (10), SAS (14), Swissair (5) and TAI (3). The Starliner's original customer base comprised TWA (29 including four from a cancelled Alitalia order), Air France (10) and Lufthansa (4) plus the unsold prototype.

Compared to its immediate predecessor, the Seven Seas featured a further 3ft 4in (1.01m) increase in fuselage length, taller vertical tail surfaces, revised operating weights with the maximum takeoff increased by a substantial 17,000lb (7,711kg) to 143,000lb (64,865kg), and more powerful 3,400hp (2,535kW) R-3350-18EA1 Turbo Compound engines.

The most significant modification was that to the wing, which until now had been basically unchanged since the DC-4. A 10ft 0in (3.05m) increase in span was introduced via a new centre section which housed additional fuel capacity, a 21 per cent increase over the DC-7B to a total of 7,824 USgal (29,617 l). The DC-7B's saddle tanks mounted in enlarged engine nacelles were retained. Weather radar was standard equipment where it had been optional on previous DC-7s and DC-6s.

The new centre section resulted in the engines being moved further outboard - providing a quieter cabin - while the increase in wing area reduced approach speeds and nullified the increased operating weights. In addition, the greater span in combination with the wing's dihedral had the effect of moving the engine thrust lines upwards, allowing the fitting of larger diameter propellers to help absorb the extra power.

The first DC-7C (N70C, c/n 44872/653) flew on 20 December 1955 and after flying with the manufacturer on tests and demonstration duties was sold to Panair do Brasil as PP-PDO in June 1957.

The DC-7C was awarded certification on 15 May 1956 and entered service with Pan American on 1 June on the trans-Atlantic route. The aircraft played a significant role in the development of international air travel in the Northern Hemisphere as it carried the lion's share of trans-Atlantic traffic until the jets entered service. It was also capable of flying a true

**France's Transports Aeriens Intercontinenteaux (TAI) purchased three new DC-7Cs including F-BIAP (c/n 45366/892) delivered in November 1957. This aircraft survived for less than two years; it was destroyed after crashing on takeoff from Bordeaux in September 1959.**

'over the North Pole' service. SAS pioneered this milestone on 24 February 1957 when it flew a DC-7C between Copenhagen and Tokyo. Other flights over the North Pole quickly followed including KLM's Amsterdam-Anchorage-Tokyo-Biak service.

The Seven Seas was the first airliner capable of tackling all the world's major land and sea barriers non stop - across the USA, the Atlantic and Pacific Oceans and over the North Pole. Several of the sectors it regularly flew took over 17 hours to complete, among them Chicago-Amsterdam, Buenos Aires-Dakar, Cairo-Capetown, Rio de Janeiro-New York and Vancouver-Tokyo. The latter was a 4,082nm (5,560km) leg which took 18hr 10min outbound against the wind and 14 hours inbound with the help of a tailwind.

The last DC-7C (PH-DSR, c/n 45549/1041 *Barents Sea*) was delivered to KLM on 10 December 1958, production of both the DC-7 and DC-6 having ended shortly beforehand. Less than six weeks earlier Pan American had inaugurated services with the Boeing 707 jet and Douglas' own DC-8 had already been undergoing flight testing for seven months. It would enter service in September 1959.

### DC-7 Turboprops

Douglas began examining the possibilities of developing turboprop versions of the DC-6/7 as early as 1951 when it looked at a DC-6A/C-118 airframe fitted with the new 2,550eshp (1,900kW) Allison T38. That concept was rejected by the US military. Other turboprop projects mooted included the use of Rolls-Royce Dart and Allison T56 engines (as fitted to the Lockheed C-130 Hercules), some based on the DC-6 and others on the DC-7.

Two of the later concepts were dubbed DC-7D (Rolls-Royce RB.109) and DC-7T (Rolls-Royce Tyne), fundamentally a turboprop DC-7C with a 40in (102cm) longer fuselage and swept vertical tail surfaces. Again, neither progressed beyond the drawing board.

### DC-7 Freighters

Once the jets entered service the DC-7C quickly became obsolete and began disappearing from the major airlines' front line fleets. As it had done with the DC-6, Douglas offered freighter or 'quick change' passenger/freight conversions of the DC-7 models in 1958, giving major operators the chance to get some more useful life out of their aircraft.

The conversion typically took about three months to perform and cost around $US350,000. It involved an installation similar to that developed for the DC-6A Liftmaster - two large freight doors on the port side fuselage, reinforced cabin floor and a freight handling system. Any standard DC-7s

**Former Pan Am DC-7C N732PA (c/n 44874/661) photographed in 1966 when operated by its fourth owner, Rhodesian based Air Trans Africa as VP-WAJ. The basic Pan Am colour scheme is still evident.**

converted were upgraded to DC-7B specifications at the same time.

Douglas performed conversions for United (six DC-7s), American (14 DC-7Bs), Panagra (one DC-7B), KLM (four DC-7Cs), BOAC (two DC-7Cs), Alitalia (two DC-7Cs) and JAL (two DC-7Cs) for a total of 31 by the manufacturer between 1959 and 1961. After conversion the aircraft were redesignated DC-7BF or DC-7CF.

Other organisations also performed freighter conversions including Lockheed Air Services which modified 13 Pan Am DC-7Cs to CF standards from 1960 using some parts supplied by Douglas. Other non factory conversions included 10 DC-7CFs for Riddle Airlines, one DC-7CF for Sabena by its own engineering division, and five DC-7CFs for Northwest.

In all, about 65 DC-7s became freighters: 20 DC-7BFs and 45 DC-7CFs. Most of these went on to have useful lives with subsequent owners and they accounted for the majority of the approximately 40 DC-7s still flying in 2001.

Apart from Pan Am, the only other US purchasers of new DC-7Cs were Braniff and Northwest, who took delivery of seven and 14, respectively. Illustrated opposite is Braniff's N5900 (c/n 45068/715).

Lockheed Air Services modified 13 Pan Am DC-7Cs to DC-7CF standards in 1959-60. This June 1961 shot of N742PA *Clipper Celestial* (c/n 44884/698) shows the rear cargo door configuration. N742PA was withdrawn from use in 1964 and stored for a year before being sold to Liberty Air (opposite).

### DOUGLAS DC-7

**Powerplants:** DC-7/7B - four 3,250hp (2,423kW) Wright R-3350-18DA-2 or DA-4 Turbo Compound 18-cylinder radials; Hamilton Standard four bladed propellers of 13ft 6in (4.11m) diameter. Fuel capacity: DC-7 - 5,512 USgal (20,865 l); DC-7B - max 6,478 USgal (24,522 l).

DC-7C - four 3,400hp (2,535kW) Wright R-3350-18EA1 Turbo Compound 18-cylinder radials; four bladed Hamilton Standard propellers of 14ft 0in (4.27m) diameter. Max fuel capacity 7,824 USgal (29,617 l).

**Dimensions:** DC-7/7B - wing span 117ft 6in (35.81m); length 108ft 11in (33.20m); height 28ft 7in (8.71m); wing area 1,463sq ft (135.9m$^2$).

DC-7C - wing span 127ft 6in (38.86m); length 112ft 3in (34.21m); height 31ft 10in (9.70m); wing area 1,637sq ft (152.1m$^2$).

**Weights:** DC-7 - empty 66,306lb (30,076kg); max takeoff 122,200lb (55,430kg); max landing 97,000lb (44,000kg); max payload 20,000lb (9,072kg).

DC-7B - empty 67,995lb (30,843kg); max takeoff 126,000lb (57,154kg); max landing 102,000lb (46,267kg); max payload 21,516lb (9,760kg).

DC-7C - empty 72,763lb (33,005kg); max takeoff 143,000lb (64,865kg); max landing 109,000lb (49,442kg); max payload 23,083lb (10,470kg).

**Accommodation:** DC-7/7B - typically 62 passengers in first class four abreast configuration or up to 99 passengers in high density layout. Baggage/freight capacity 651cu ft (18.4m$^3$) in two underfloor holds.

DC-7C - 62-105 passengers depending on configuration. Standard baggage/freight capacity 651cu ft (18.4m$^3$) and 13,440lb (6,096kg) in two underfloor holds; optional 954cu ft (27.0m$^3$) and 18,100lb (8,210kg).

**Performance:** DC-7 - max cruise 312kt (577km/h); takeoff to 50ft 6,060ft (1,847m); max payload range (no reserves) 2,476nm (4,587km); max fuel range (no reserves) 3,770nm (6,983km).

DC-7B - max cruise 313kt (580km/h); takeoff to 50ft 6,350ft (1,935m); max payload range (no reserves) 2,850nm (5,279km); max fuel range (no reserves) 4,275nm (7,918km).

DC-7C - max speed 331kt (613km/h) at 22,000ft; max cruise 304kt (563km/h) at 23,300ft; takeoff distance to 50ft 6,400ft (1,950m); max payload range (no reserves) 4,000nm (7,409km); max fuel range (no reserves) 4,900nm (9,076km).

# APPENDICES

## Summary of Deliveries

Notes: The table summarises actual DC-6 and DC-7 deliveries to initial customers (including military), noting the operator, model, quantity, date of first delivery and pertinent notes. It does not cover resales but does include two DC-7Bs which crashed before delivery, one each intended for Continental and Eastern.

| Customer | Model | Qty | 1st Deliv | Notes |
|---|---|---|---|---|
| Aerolineas Argentinas | DC-6 | 6 | May 1948 | |
| Aerolineas Peruanas | DC-6A | 1 | May 1958 | |
| Aigle Azur | DC-6B | 1 | Aug 1955 | |
| Air Liban | DC-6A | 1 | Oct 1957 | |
| | DC-6C | 1 | June 1958 | |
| Alaska Airlines | DC-6A | 1 | Oct 1958 | |
| Alitalia/LAI | DC-6 | 4 | Sept 1950 | |
| | DC-6B | 10 | Nov 1953 | 1 cvtd to DC-6BF, 1 to DC-6A/B |
| | DC-7C | 6 | Oct 1957 | 2 cvtd to DC-7CF |
| American Airlines | DC-6 | 50 | Nov 1946 | 5 cvtd to DC-6F |
| | DC-6A | 10 | May 1953 | 2 cvtd to DC-6A/B |
| | DC-6B | 25 | April 1951 | 1 cvtd to DC-6BF, 4 to DC-6A/B |
| | DC-7 | 34 | Oct 1953 | |
| | DC-7B | 24 | March 1956 | 12 cvtd to DC-7BF |
| Aramco | DC-6A | 1 | Aug 1956 | |
| | DC-6B | 2 | July 1952 | |
| Australian National Airways | DC-6B | 4 | Feb 1955 | |
| Belgian Air Force | DC-6A | 2 | May 1958 | |
| BOAC | DC-7C | 10 | Oct 1956 | 2 cvtd to DC-7CF |
| Braniff Airways | DC-6 | 9 | Aug 1947 | 1 cvtd to DC-6F |
| | DC-7C | 7 | Sept 1956 | |
| British C'wealth Pacific | DC-6 | 4 | Sept 1948 | |
| Canadian Pacific Airlines | DC-6A | 6 | Sept 1953 | |
| | DC-6B | 13 | Jan 1953 | 3 cvtd to DC-6BF, 2 to DC-6A/B |
| Cathay Pacific | DC-6B | 1 | June 1958 | |
| Civil Air Transport | DC-6B | 1 | Sept 1958 | cvtd to DC-6A/B |
| Continental Air Lines | DC-6B | 2 | March 1953 | 1 cvtd to DC-6BF |
| | DC-7B | 6 | March 1957 | 1 crashed before delivery |
| Delta Air Lines | DC-6 | 7 | Sept 1948 | |
| | DC-7 | 10 | Feb 1954 | |
| | DC-7B | 11 | Dec 1955 | |
| Eastern Air Lines | DC-7B | 50 | June 1955 | 1 crashed before delivery |
| Ethiopian Airlines | DC-6B | 3 | April 1958 | |
| Flying Tiger Line | DC-6A | 8 | Aug 1953 | to JAL (2), Northwest (4), Lockheed (1) |
| Hunting Clan Air Transport | DC-6C | 2 | Aug 1958 | |
| Japan Air Lines | DC-6B | 2 | Sept 1954 | |
| | DC-7C | 4 | Dec 1957 | 2 cvtd to DC-7CF |
| Jugoslav Aerotransport | DC-6B | 2 | Oct 1958 | |
| KLM Royal Dutch | DC-6 | 8 | April 1948 | 2 cvtd to DC-6F |
| | DC-6A | 2 | July 1953 | |
| | DC-6B | 7 | May 1952 | |
| | DC-7C | 15 | April 1957 | 4 cvtd to DC-7CF |
| LAN Chile | DC-6B | 6 | Jan 1955 | 1 cvtd to DC-6BF |
| Loide Aereo Nacional | DC-6C | 4 | Dec 1958 | |

| Customer | Model | Qty | 1st Deliv | Notes |
|---|---|---|---|---|
| Maritime Central Airways | DC-6A | 1 | June 1958 | |
| | DC-6B | 1 | July 1958 | |
| Mexicana | DC-6 | 3 | Nov 1950 | |
| | DC-6B | 2 | June 1953 | |
| | DC-7C | 3 | March 1957 | 1 cvtd to DC-7CF |
| National Airlines | DC-6 | 5 | Oct 1947 | 1 cvtd to DC-6F |
| | DC-6B | 8 | Oct 1952 | 1 cvtd to DC-6BF |
| | DC-7 | 4 | Nov 1953 | |
| | DC-7B | 4 | Oct 1957 | |
| Nevada Aero Trades | DC-6A | 2 | June 1958 | lsd to Great Lakes Airlines |
| North American Airlines | DC-6B | 2 | Dec 1954 | both cvtd to DC-6A/B |
| Northeast Airlines | DC-6B | 10 | Jan 1957 | 7 cvtd to DC-6BF |
| Northwest Orient | DC-6A | 1 | Feb 1956 | |
| | DC-6B | 12 | June 1955 | 2 cvtd to DC-6BF |
| | DC-7C | 14 | Feb 1957 | 10 cvtd to DC-7CF |
| Olympic Airways | DC-6B | 4 | July 1958 | 1 cvtd to DC-6BF |
| Overseas National Airways | DC-6A | 3 | Feb 1958 | |
| Panair do Brasil | DC-7C | 4 | June 1957 | |
| Pan American Airways | DC-6A | 4 | May 1954 | |
| | DC-6B | 45 | Feb 1952 | 11 cvtd to DC-6A/B, 7 to DC-6BF |
| | DC-7B | 7 | May 1955 | |
| | DC-7C | 26 | April 1956 | 15 cvtd to DC-7CF |
| Pan American Grace | DC-6 | 6 | March 1947 | |
| | DC-6B | 4 | April 1952 | |
| | DC-7B | 6 | June 1955 | 1 cvtd to DC-7BF |
| Philippine Air Lines | DC-6 | 5 | April 1948 | |
| | DC-6B | 2 | June 1952 | |
| Riddle Airlines | DC-6A | 1 | Nov 1957 | to Hughes Tool Co |
| Sabena | DC-6 | 5 | July 1947 | |
| | DC-6A | 2 | May 1954 | |
| | DC-6B | 9 | March 1953 | 2 cvtd to DC-6A/B |
| | DC-7C | 10 | Nov 1956 | 2 cvtd to DC-7CF |
| SAS | DC-6 | 13 | May 1948 | |
| | DC-6B | 14 | May 1952 | 1 cvtd to DC-6BF |
| | DC-7C | 4 | Aug 1956 | 4 cvtd to DC-7CF |
| Slick Airways | DC-6A | 11 | April 1951 | 1 each to Alaska Airlines, Eagle Aviation, Overseas National Airlines |
| South African Airways | DC-7B | 4 | Feb 1956 | 1 cvtd to DC-7BF |
| Swissair | DC-6A | 1 | Oct 1958 | |
| | DC-6B | 6 | June 1951 | |
| | DC-7C | 5 | Nov 1956 | 3 cvtd to DC-7CF |
| TAI | DC-6B | 5 | April 1953 | |
| | DC-7C | 3 | Nov 1957 | |
| Trans American Airlines | DC-6B | 5 | Dec 1956 | 3 cvtd to DC-6A/B |
| Trans Caribbean Airlines | DC-6A | 3 | Nov 1957 | |
| United Airlines | DC-6 | 48 | March 1947 | 2 cvtd to DC-6F |
| | DC-6A | 7 | April 1956 | |
| | DC-6B | 44 | April 1951 | 4 cvtd to DC-6BF, 3 to DC-6A/B |
| | DC-7 | 57 | April 1954 | 6 cvtd to DC-7F |
| US Air Force | C-118 | 1 | July 1947 | |
| | C-118A | 101 | July 1952 | |
| US Navy | R6D-1 | 65 | Nov 1951 | redesignated C-118B, 38 to USAF as C-118A |
| UTA | DC-6B | 2 | March 1958 | |
| Western Air Lines | DC-6B | 31 | Nov 1952 | 5 cvtd to DC-6A/B, 8 to DC-6BF |

## Constructor's Numbers

Douglas used a continuous sequence of constructor's numbers (c/n) regardless of aircraft type and also a series of line numbers (l/n) for the DC-6/7, this a 'factory' or 'fuselage' number shared between the two models and indicating their close relationship.

The first true DC-6 (excluding the XC-112A prototype) was c/n 42854 (l/n 1) and the last - a DC-6B - was c/n 45564 (l/n 1040). DC-7 numbers ranged from c/n 44122 (l/n 350) for the first aircraft through to c/n 45553 (l/n 1038), although the last aircraft given a line number (1041) was c/n 45549. The XC-112A had c/n 36326 and no line number.

There were a couple of anomalies: line number 1A was allocated to DC-6 c/n 43061, and line number 173 (c/n 43220) was not used. as the DC-6 to which it was allocated was not built.

## US Military Serial Numbers

**XC-112A:** 45-0873.
**C-118:** 46-0505.
**C-118A:** 50-1843/50-1844; 51-3818/51-3835; 51-17626/51-17661; 51-17667/51-17668; 53-3223/53-3305 (includes transfers from USN).
**R6D-1/C-118B:** BuAer 128423-128433; 131567-131620; 152687-152689; 153691-153694 (includes transfers from USAF).

| Production Summary | |
|---|---:|
| XC-112A | 1 |
| DC-6 | 174 |
| DC-6A | 67 |
| DC-6C | 7 |
| DC-6B | 288 |
| C-118 | 1 |
| C-118A | 101 |
| R6D-1/C-118B | 65 |
| **Total DC-6** | **704** |
| DC-7 | 105 |
| DC-7B | 112 |
| DC-7C | 121 |
| **Total DC-7** | **338** |
| **Overall total** | **1042** |

New Zealand's TEAL's (the forerunner of today's Air New Zealand) purchased three DC-6s from British Commonwealth Pacific Airways in 1954 for Pacific and trans-Tasman services. All three were sold to the RNZAF in 1961.

Former National Airlines DC-6 N90894 (c/n 43058/86) in the colours of its third owner, Nicaragua's LANICA as AN-AMI. This shot was taken in September 1965 and the aircraft was converted to a DC-6F freighter in 1969.

| | **DC-6 and DC-7 Annual Deliveries** | | |
|---|---|---|---|
| | (all models including military) | | |
| Year | DC-6 | DC-7 | Total |
| 1946 | 7 | - | 7 |
| 1947 | 92 | - | 92 |
| 1948 | 50 | - | 50 |
| 1949 | 3 | - | 3 |
| 1950 | 17 | - | 17 |
| 1951 | 37 | - | 37 |
| 1952 | 96 | - | 96 |
| 1953 | 116 | 12 | 128 |
| 1954 | 60 | 48 | 108 |
| 1955 | 75 | 27 | 102 |
| 1956 | 41 | 70 | 111 |
| 1957 | 44 | 124 | 168 |
| 1958 | 65 | 55 | 120 |
| 1959 | 1 | - | 1 |
| **Totals** | **704** | ***336** | ***1040** |

\* 2 DC-7Bs written off before delivery excluded, 1 each in 1957 and 1958

DC-7B firebomber N838D (c/n 45347/936) of Thompson Flying Services started life in February 1958 as one of the 50 delivered to Eastern Air Lines. Thompson purchased the aircraft in August 1968.

# DC-6 Models

by

High Quality 1:200 scale models of Douglas DC-6/6B aircraft as featured in this publication:

← Manufactured in Australia to agency model specification
← Simple snap together assembly, complete with stand
← Solid fuselages
← Full printed wing detail
← Decalled and oversprayed in a clear gloss lacquer
← Accurate artwork generated by Juanita Franzi, and other globally recognised aviation graphic artists
← Models generally restricted to limited runs

Illustrated are our Cathay Pacific, Delta, Panagra, British Eagle and Pan American DC-6 models.

Douglas and DC-6 are registered trade marks of the Boeing Commercial Airplane Group and are used under licence.

Visit our secure website www.modelair.com.au to look at the Douglas DC-6 and other aircraft models and prototypes of models in production in the Nostalgair™ and Modelair™ range.

## MODELAIR Pty Ltd

P.O. Box C19, Werrington County, NSW 2747, AUSTRALIA.
Tel +61 2 4722 5670     Fax +61 2 4730 3342     Email: modelair@tpg.com.au